For Sue and Rod —

Happy Holidays!

Thicker

Dec. 2003

for Joe and Rachel
Happy Holidays
...
Dec. 2003

Diether H. Haenicke

Wednesdays with Diether

Opinions, Observations, and Reminiscences
from his weekly Gazette column

Edited by

Kurt R. Haenicke

Foreword

When I approached Diether Haenicke four years ago with a proposal to write weekly columns for the Gazette, I was certain he would be very good at it. From years of listening to him in action as president of Western Michigan University, I knew how quick, witty and insightful he could be in extemporaneous speech. I also knew he possessed opinions about almost every imaginable topic, and was willing to express his views with unusual candor. In other words: a natural newspaper columnist. Hundreds of Wednesday columns later, I realize that Diether has done even better than I could have hoped. His graceful writing has introduced thousands of people in Southwest Michigan, on a very personal level, to one of their community's finest minds and healthiest perspectives on life. Many readers tell me they first turn to his essay when their Wednesday newspaper arrives.

In selecting 91 of his columns for inclusion in this single volume, his son Kurt has organized them into sections that are more than the sum of their episodic parts. Read by section, they gain a different texture and become coherent commentaries on higher education, on language, on growing up in wartime Germany, and especially on the simple wonders and travails of being alive and human. Taken together, the columns constitute a memoir of a different kind. When Diether writes about the indignity of wearing an open hospital gown, or the joy of grandchildren, or about aging and exercise, or keeping work in perspective, or concerning irritations of poor customer service, readers can find their own feelings about life put beautifully, and often hilariously, into words.

In these pages one can learn of the hooker-educator Amalia, watch Diether and his wonderful wife Carol practice ballroom dancing in their garage, come along with a young boy as he smuggles butter to barter for piano strings on the black market of post-war Germany, and meet wonderfully talented (and not-so-wonderfully talented) students of WMU.

My favorite section of the book deals with Diether's memories of his childhood in Germany during the 1940s, and his reflections on this period. This is a time often analyzed in terms of its tragic military and political events, but which is much less often described through simple childhood memories. One can meet his family, and vicariously share a glass of mulled red wine with them. Or one can go with Diether on his search for records of his town's vanished pre-war synagogues and read of ordinary townspeople who screened off their memories of the Holocaust. It is enough to give caution to people in all times and all places. When Diether compares Hitler's cult of personality to that of Saddam Hussein's, it carries a chill of authenticity.

Diether's German upbringing, of course, is an intrinsic part of Dr. Haenicke's adult Kalamazoo persona. His accent, after 40 years in America, is distinctive. Don't miss the anecdote about his conversation with the similarly accented Henry Kissinger, when both switched to German so they could understand each other. His name is also the most frequently mispronounced in Southwest Michigan, even by people who ought to know better, including sometimes those introducing him in public. Yet I have never heard him complain or correct someone. I can remember several occasions on which I quietly would correct a dinner companion who had just butchered Diether's family name. I would write out HEN-ICK-A on a napkin for them, accenting the first syllable with my very best sketch of a hen, feathers and all, as a memory aid for them in the future.

I think fondly of Diether's accent and his distinctive Germanness because they define the journey of this immensely talented man. If America's story is the story of immigrant families (two of my grandparents came to America on a boat as well), then Diether's life explains a great deal about how this nation has been so successful at welcoming wonderfully gifted people from around the world, allowing them to keep their distinctive heritages, yet giving them opportunity without limit, including the chance to lead our most important institutions. As any reader of this book will know, Diether has not led a German-American life, but a quintessential American life.

In one of the humorous anecdotes in the pages that follow, a student, with language challenges of his own, thanks Diether: "Dr. Haenicke," he said, "I learned so much in your class. You helped me infinitesimally." Well, Diether, you've helped us a lot more than infinitesimally, not only through your outstanding presidency at Western Michigan University, but in helping us see ourselves and the world more clearly through the wisdom and good humor of your columns.

—George Arwady

Table of Contents

I. On Campus:
Notes from the Ivory Tower

II. English as a Second Language:
Observations of an Immigrant Nitpicker

III. As I see it:
Observations, Opinions, and Anecdotes

IV. Memories:
Of Times and Places Past

Christmas Memories:

I. On Campus:

Notes from the Ivory Tower

Disgusted in Oshtemo

Every public official receives bundles of curious correspondence. During my years as a university president, I was frequently praised for accomplishments that were not my own—but with similar regularity I was chided for actions taken by others without any involvement on my side. I guess that comes with the territory.

I collected some of the letters that I received during my public life and will share one of many. (The names have been changed to protect the innocent.)

To: Office of the President
Western Michigan University
President Haenicke or current resident

To Whom It May Concern:

I am still totally upset because of an incident that occurred last Wednesday at the intersection of Stadium Drive and Howard Street.

As I was driving home on Stadium Drive, I had to wait in front of a red light. While my car was stopped, five Western students standing on the loading area of a pickup truck pulled down their pants and bared their rear ends right into my face. Although I could not see their faces due to the fact that my car window is much lower than the truck bed, I heard the students laugh at their disgusting display.

For me this is no laughing matter. Instead I find such behavior utterly disgusting. And you, Mr. President, should be ashamed about the behavior of your students. They are a disgrace to our community. I blame you for not doing anything about it.

Signed: Disgusted in Oshtemo, Mrs. Catery

I sent the following reply:

Dear Mrs. Catery:

Your letter is in front of me, addressed 'to whom it may concern,' or 'to the current resident' of my office. While it is certain that I am, at this moment, still the current resident, I am not equally convinced that I am the one to whom your problem should be a real concern.

What you described was called 'mooning' when I was young. I thought the practice went out in the late sixties when total, not just partial nudity, as in mooning, entered the mainstream of theatrical events and the acts of performance artists.

I don't know whether I should be ashamed, as you suggest, that the younger generation has rediscovered the same joys of tasteless and sophomoric entertainment in which some of their parents used to indulge. In general, though, I tend to be quite proud of our Western students and relatively tolerant of certain exuberant youthful behavior, as long as it is not vicious, dangerous, or hurtful to others.

Nevertheless, you were disgusted, and I am most sorry to hear that, and I offer my sincere apologies.

However, I am puzzled by one question. If indeed you could not see the persons' faces but only those anatomical areas that so disgusted you, how could you tell that you were exposed to students, and Western students in particular? Is there a common denominator that identifies certain rear end features as those of Western students?

If we ever develop a student ID system at the university and are looking for identification features in addition to fingerprints and full face photos, we may look to you for expert advice.

With regards and apologies,
Diether Haenicke
Current Resident

April 14, 1999

∾

Painful Moments at Commencements

I must have attended, as provost or president of three universities, at least several hundred commencement exercises. This particular academic ceremony held its charm for me throughout the years, and I never became blasé about it. I always loved the exuberance of the graduates, and vicariously I felt each time the unbridled parental pride which also had overcome me when my own two children were graduated.

At Wayne State University, we conducted graduations in giant Cobo Hall, a ceremony to which half of Detroit seemed to show up. At Ohio State, in the historic football stadium, fifty thousand relatives needed field glasses to spot their eight thousand offspring file across the gridiron at summer commencement. At Western Michigan, we made the ceremony more intimate by holding it in the festively decorated Miller Auditorium. Multiple graduation exercises on the same day made it possible for all students to bring numerous guests, and each graduate would receive a personal handshake and the diploma from the hand of the president.

While the personal handshakes may have made a difference to the students, they always took the greatest toll on me. Having successively squeezed the hands of two thousand students plus those of a few hundred enthusiastic relatives from 9 a.m. to 4 p.m., I would often throw off my academic robes, race home, and spend the evenings soaking my right hand in a bucket of ice water. For many students, commencement was their one and only personal encounter with the university president, and they did their best to make it memorable. Many a Michigan farm boy threw his entire macho manhood into the encounter and turned the handshake into an assault with a deadly weapon. I feared particularly the ROTC cadets who had been taught that a good military handshake resembles a viselike grip. My wide open eyes and the broad grin I displayed were sometimes not expressions of cheerfulness but a reflection of the extreme pain enthusiastically inflicted on me by the cadets. These men and women, I felt, were ready for hand-to-hand combat.

However, once in a while someone came along who had been taught neither by mother nor military how to shake hands. A limp, dangling extremity was extended towards me, and as I took it I felt I was touching a dripping wet towel. The wet towel students usually received an additional pat on the shoulder, which might have suggested to the astounded parents a special cordiality between president and student. In reality, I simply needed the student's shoulder to dry off my hand before the next person in line grabbed it again.

Other students preferred not to have their hands shaken at all. Occasionally, I was visited prior to commencement by a delegation of international students, all of them men, who very politely advised me that their customs do not allow strange men to touch any part of a woman's body. This precaution was to avoid male sexual arousal. Would I please dispense with the handshake for the women in their group and simply hand them their diplomas? Of course I complied with their wishes. When the women then passed by, completely hidden from head to toe under disguising dark clothes, with only the eyes barely visible, I felt flattered that anyone would think that at my age I could possibly be aroused by a mere touch of their hands. Seldom have I been so overestimated.

To this day, I keep running into students who come up to me and tell me that they shook my hand at commencement, and that they enjoyed the ceremony. Just the other day, a friendly fellow in Detroit assured me: "You gave me a wonderful piece of advice during commencement that I will never forget." I was touched that I should have made such a lasting impact on a student and asked him: "What was the advice I gave you?" He replied: "When I stood in front of you and shook your hand, I hesitated for a moment, and you said to me: 'Move on, son!' I have followed that advice ever since."

June 6, 2001

~

Are finals week and Judgment Day one and the same?

The telephone keeps ringing, the email overflows, for the first time during the semester my office hours are really busy—it is finals week. Only a few more nights before the last exam; and just as in the Bible: the sins of the past haunt the sinner on Judgment Day, and there is much howling and gnashing of teeth. A few nights of cramming won't make up for solid, regular study throughout the semester. Therefore, one after another sleep-deprived and irrationally hopeful student shows up at my doorstep seeking belated guidance towards a passing grade. Others seek an audience to offer examples of outstanding contemporary fiction as to what afflictions and what incomparable blows of fate have befallen them during the semester. Others yet turn the office into a confessional and freely admit their sins, pleading for forgiveness.

I love the stories my students invent or embellish. Most are better than the ones I remember from my own student days. But my students deal with a teacher of literature who, while he loves a good story, also recognizes fiction when he sees it. I am less comfortable in the confessional. While I am great at forgiveness, I don't have the power to absolve the sinners and must remind them that I give grades, not absolution.

It is remarkable how many students think that teachers can 'give' them a grade just to be of help. They point an accusing finger at the professor and reveal that all scholarship support will be lost, they will be made destitute, if the insensitive and cold-hearted instructor does not dole out the needed grade. But I don't go on guilt trips for which I haven't booked passage myself, and I certainly don't take any responsibility if my students' laziness leads to their loss of money.

Other students think grades are a negotiable commodity. They put on their best salesmen faces, fully convinced that a win-win situation can be developed if both parties are willing to deal. A particularly insistent one told me that President Floyd had declared Western a "student-centered" university. Would I please be more accommodating? To the student's credit, though, his remark was tongue in cheek. As the old joke goes: "What's the difference between a professor and a terrorist?" Answer: "You can negotiate with a terrorist."

I agree that we make perhaps too much of testing and grades. But a grade is a professional judgment, a seal of quality. By giving a grade, I attest to the student's ability to perform on a given level. I am telling a future employer or a graduate or professional school how well this student has mastered a given subject. That's why there can be neither negotiation nor absolution.

Thank heavens, most students do not need to resort to deals, confession, or fiction to end the semester with a good grade. I am always impressed with the fact that most of them behave very responsibly and are determined to do well academically. They make my work in the classroom a pleasure, and I feel rewarded when the academic outcome of a semester results in good grades for my students.

But even those who struggle academically, play too much, don't find their focus in their freshman year, or who need a lot of help and guidance, have my full attention—perhaps even more than those who sail through their four years of undergraduate work without shipwreck. My friend Kathy Brady often remarks: "Everybody is someone's little boy or girl." I love that motherly observation because it reminds me that we are not only teachers but also parents and would like our own children treated with love and understanding by others. The older I get and the longer I teach, the more I have come to believe that those who teach must love those whom they teach. And that includes tough love and bad grades, if necessary.

December 13, 2000

∾

When young freshmen put old professors in their places

All teachers have stories to tell about their students. A few bad ones, yes, but good ones usually. Any teacher who really loves teaching must also love those whom he instructs, and thus all stories about one's students tend to have a strong undercurrent of affection.

I confess to a special preference for teaching undergraduates, incoming freshmen in particular. They are still wide-eyed during their first year on campus, struggling with their new-found freedom from home, adjusting to many new responsibilities, tempted by a host of unexpected experiences, and charting their way into a broad and often overwhelming academic territory.

Their newness makes freshmen often strikingly naïve which, in turn, makes me most forgiving. Naïveté has its charm; of course only if it does not remain a constant state of mind. But certain freshman questions are disarmingly unsophisticated. I prepare most conscientiously for each class and try to make each session count; so it baffles me when a student asks: "I am sorry I couldn't come to class on Monday. Did I miss anything? Did we discuss anything important?" I am always tempted to assure the student ironically that nothing important is ever discussed in my classes, but I fear I might be believed and hesitate to run that risk. What the student actually wants to know is if anything discussed on Monday will be found on the final exam—which makes it important. A teacher has to learn that.

And freshmen indicate that they have their priorities right. How else should one interpret the not infrequent statement: "I have a real important test in marketing today; so I hope you don't mind if I leave your class early." That puts the teacher of drama and poetry in his place. Important stuff comes first, yessir!

When I teach a foreign language course, the material is highly structured—much like a math course where one can't leave out multiplication or addition and still expect to advance to the next level without severe complications. The structured approach and repetitive oral pattern drills make regular attendance not only advisable but mandatory. But I have seen students who, after missing ten out of twenty sessions, approach me shortly before their final with the hopeful question: "What can I do to make up for what I have missed?" The answer to this question borders on the religious, since all the student can offer at that point is penance and vows of self-improvement. But it is too late to obtain academic redemption. And still he raises the totally unrealistic question: "But what if I ace the final?" Is that naïveté, or what? How could that possibly happen? "Hope springs eternal in the human breast," muses the teacher of poetry.

But there is also gratitude—sort of. Once, after having dwelled a whole semester on the Latin and Greek roots in much of the English lexicon, a student expressed his appreciation thusly: "Dr. Haenicke, I learned so much in your class. You helped me infinitesimally." I dared not suggest that he might mean 'infinitely.' How was I to know if his own assessment of the situation was not, indeed, more accurate?

The ultimate let-down occurred at the end of the last winter term. A very nice freshman in my class came up to me one day to reveal a discovery he had just made. He said to me: "Do you know there is a building on campus named after a guy with the same name as yours?" This time I was probably the naïve one. Thirteen long years I was president of this university and thought that this fact would be remembered for some time. Obviously not by freshmen. *Sic transit gloria mundi!*

May 24, 2000

~

Is dressing with respect gone?

Elizabeth Kutsche, a devoted and exacting reader of the *Gazette* and an occasional correspondent of mine, wrote to me a few weeks ago. She was not amused. The paper had published a front-page article about grade inflation in American colleges, and a picture of me teaching undergraduates accompanied the story. Several readers assumed that my picture was chosen as a glaring example of one who has succumbed to the trend of throwing easy grades into the student crowd quicker than you can say A plus. But Ms. Kutsche had looked at the picture more closely and wrote in dismay: "Dear Dr. Haenicke, say it isn't so?! A hat in class? And even more unbelievable, in *your* class?! Is dressing with respect gone?"

What caused her consternation? The press photo showed Tom Busch, one of my students, with a red baseball cap on his head, the visor turned backwards, as is the absurd but accepted fashion of the day. Tom studied with me for two semesters and was one of my best students in both courses. He is a bright, polite, and conscientious young man—the kind of student one wishes to have more of in every class. Keeping his cap on certainly meant no disrespect. And the fact that I did not consider his headgear unusual shows that dress codes in university classes have changed dramatically and for good. Though not for the better, I must agree with Ms. Kutsche.

Archival class photos of the early days at Western show every young man sporting tie and coat and the young co-eds uniformly clad in dresses. No trousers for the women; mostly high collars on dresses or blouses. And no distracting cleavage. When venturing into town, proper young ladies wore white gloves and hats. That's what the archives show. However, even in my own student days—not quite that long ago—I wore a tie and jacket to class, and a hat on my head during lectures would have been unthinkable. But in those days, my professors also dressed up. I can't remember ever having seen any one of them without a suit and a tie.

The late sixties brought major changes. Students rebelled worldwide against all sorts of established rules, and many professors, especially the younger ones, joined their ranks. I remember faculty meetings at Wayne State University for which some professors dressed professionally while others were indistinguishable from urban guerillas. Colleagues, who had not spent a single day in the armed forces, nevertheless came to class in army fatigues, thus demonstrating their militancy regarding all social issues. Beards memorializing political grandfather Marx sprouted throughout the social science and humanities departments, signaling the wearers' radical orientation rather than emphasizing their masculinity. During my years in Detroit, I could, almost without fail, tell the younger faculty members' discipline by their dress and facial hair. By and large, business, engineering, and medical faculty dressed conventionally and shaved regularly. Many members of the other faculties did not and took pride in looking like unmade beds.

Dressing down has now become a national trend. Even businesses have succumbed. On 'Casual Fridays' I wonder whether I have entered a local bank or stepped out on Montego Bay.

Dot.com entrepreneurs, young and unconventional all, introduced blue jeans, T-shirts, and sneakers to the boardroom. Male fashion models have given up shaving, because three to five day stubble is the new epitome of sex appeal. Don Johnson taught a whole generation that attending formal events without socks and tie was the 'in' thing. For years now, basketball players play in the most ill-fitting and sloppy uniforms since the beginning of the sport.

I think many people consider dressing down as just being comfortable, and consider dresses, ties, and socks as choking societal straightjackets. I am not judging them. But given the professorial example regarding dress code, I don't mind that Tom Busch keeps his cap on during my class. Moreover, I have it on good authority that the younger generation considers the turned around baseball cap part of the male anatomy.

May 9, 2001

∽

Universities should not behave like corporate America

President Bush took off the gloves and promised a frontal attack on the excesses committed by American business leaders and their corporate boards. Some of them, he pointed out, are completely out of touch with the world in which their own employees, their customers, and their shareholders live. While dismissing employees by the tens of thousands, boards heaped bonuses, options, and exorbitant salaries on executives before they steered their companies into bankruptcies. Mainstream America, seeing its investments dwindle, stands with its mouth agape as it watches this unbelievable, obscene spectacle.

But corporate America is getting the point. It is for certain that employment contracts with new executives will be more carefully crafted, and that any unconscionable largesse of boards will be sharply criticized in the future.

However, one big segment of our society is not yet with the program. The greed, insensitivity, and outright callousness that brought on the downfall of public trust in corporations seems still well and alive in some university boardrooms. I almost fell off my chair when I read the other day that the newly elected president of the University of Tennessee was receiving a compensation package of $600,000 in his first year. Only days later the papers reported that the same University of Tennessee had to suspend operations for a week because of a severe state budget crisis.

I had hardly digested this absurd coincidence when I read that the new chancellor at the University of Texas had just signed on with a compensation package of $800,000 which makes him possibly the highest-paid university leader—private universities included—in the country. He thus exceeds even the compensation of the president of Dowling College (anyone ever heard of that school?) who took home $788,000.

Our students are shouldering enormous annual tuition increases, at times exceeding 10%. Each public university in the universe claims to be severely underfunded. Every alum under the sun gets pleading messages to send money to the starving alma mater. What is happening here?

There is a reason for this unfortunate discrepancy between claims of institutional poverty and presidential pay. Many university trustees, usually from business backgrounds, no longer view universities as centers of education and academic inquiry but as businesses. Presidents, formerly intellectual leaders of their institutions, have become CEOs who do not guide universities but who manage corporate enterprises. Many trustees argue that, if presidents are not extravagantly paid, they will leave for greener pastures, thus making presidents look like migrant moneygrubbers instead of institution builders.

I don't understand the new breed of college presidents who want to be CEOs. I consider those of us who serve in state universities as public officials, who already draw salaries that exceed those of most other public servants. In fact, we are usually paid more than the governor, who presides over a much larger and much more complex enterprise. We live, free of charge, in beautiful homes. We travel all over the world, usually at the expense of the institution. We enjoy the services of large staffs, drive university-owned cars, and seldom ever have to open our private wallets when a bill arrives. We have every reason to be satisfied with current salaries that reflect our status as public servants and that are much higher than we ever expected when we started out as young assistant professors. The job is demanding and difficult, and presidents should be well paid; but there is a line between good pay and appropriate benefits and wretched excess. In Tennessee and Texas that line has been crossed.

Corporate-level compensation is inappropriate in tax-exempt state institutions with charitable tax status. If larger paychecks are needed anywhere, they are needed for the hordes of part-timers who slave away in our universities. If excess funds are available, boards should spend them on more faculty positions, better staff salaries, or larger stipends for students. University boards that only recently had to levy immense, back-breaking tuition increases; boards that cannot provide better than very modest pay increases for staff and faculty, should think twice before they heap lavish compensation packages on college CEOs. Boards must learn that universities are first and foremost not businesses. They must, truly must learn from the mistakes of corporate America.

July 17, 2002

∾

Family support is essential to a student's success

I had dinner with two graduating seniors who, in a few days, would walk across the stage in Miller Auditorium to receive their bachelor's degrees. One of them, Vanessa Bodnar, had written a senior thesis entitled "The Use of Indomethacin to Prevent Heterotopic Ossification Following Operative Treatment of Acetabular Fractures." The other one, Michael Dozeman, would begin work for Stryker Instruments right after graduation. For his senior project he chose work on a "Memory Chip Emulator for Surgical Power Tools." These are undergraduates, mind you. Had the dinner conversation focused on these student topics, it would have been very one-sided. But luckily, the dinner had a different purpose. The WMU Medallion Program had invited parents and sponsors to celebrate the young scholars who entered the program in 1997 and who would soon be graduated.

The Medallion Program is a remarkable WMU institution. Born about twenty years ago on President John Bernhard's watch, it attracts annually hundreds of gifted students who compete for the two dozen full-ride undergraduate scholarships, now each worth $32,000. The scholarships are awarded strictly on merit. The selection committee tries to select those students who show the highest academic promise coupled with potential for leadership and a concern for social issues.

Anyone pessimistic about today's youth should have observed, as I did, these young men and women as they recalled their undergraduate experience at Western Michigan University. They represented the full range of academic majors: the hard sciences, the arts and humanities, but also engineering and education. I remembered many of the students from when I first welcomed them to the university in the fall of 1997. What a difference the four years made! I particularly recall Mike Dozeman—whose scholarship bears Carol's and my name—then a lanky, semi-shy entering freshman and now a full-grown, focused, worldly, and confident young man ready for a professional career. He made us proud.

After dinner, the Medallion Scholars rose to take leave from their friends and their undergraduate years. They spoke about their academic fields, but mainly about friendships forged, frustrations encountered, the good times to be remembered, the occasional tears shed, the love received from family and friends, and finally about the bittersweet joy of leaving and facing graduate or professional school or 'real life' in the workplace. Their brief and often humorous remarks should be reminders for all commencement speakers that brevity and poignancy make the best speeches. We were reminded what a great deal of living and learning goes on outside the classroom during those undergraduate years. The students encouraged one another to reach out to different people: for the wallflower to befriend the seemingly odd classmate with multiple body piercings and blue hair, and for the artistic one to befriend the nerd. Others, mostly in theatre, creative writing, or music, thanked their parents for having let them go their own unconventional ways and for allowing them a broad, 'impractical,' liberal education. I was impressed by the students' academic achievements, but I was touched by their caring for one another and by the unembarrassed expression of love for their families. Only the unbounded pride and fondness of their families matched the warmth with which the students spoke of parents, siblings, and loved ones.

Here lies, in my opinion, a central aspect for all educational success. Without a loving family's interest and its constant emotional support, few students succeed. Teachers are critical in a student's advancement, no doubt, but they are only effective in partnership with the learner's home environment. To succeed academically and to grow into a good, responsible adult, a student needs love and support from home. These students certainly all had this irreplaceable advantage.

After an evening like this one, I stop worrying—for a while at least—about the future. I look at these young people and know that our political, our social, our economic, and academic institutions will be in good hands. Being in their midst, I am reminded again why I have always loved being a teacher, and I go home knowing that "God's in his heaven, all's right with the world!"

April 4, 2001

∾

Football, the sport of college presidents

During the decades I spent in universities that played sports on the Division I level, not a single year passed in which I lived without nagging worries about college athletics. I am a great fan of college sports and like nothing better than watching a gridiron contest on a glorious fall day or attending basketball, baseball, volleyball, and ice hockey games. But I could never look without serious concern at the rampant commercialization of college sports, the run-away coaches' salaries, the illicit betting, the dismal graduation rates of many teams, the incessant rules violations, and the illegal payments to star players.

Realizing that I often reflected on the role of athletics in universities, my friend and colleague Harold "Hal" Ray directed my attention to the book, *Saga of American Sports* (1978), which sheds some interesting light on the history of college athletics. Interestingly, the recruitment of students for extracurricular activities did not start with sports. It started with gaining pledges from high school students to join the debating societies which were the primary arena of competitive activity among colleges prior to athletics. Academic purists may bemoan the fact that an oratorical and essentially intellectual activity was replaced by muscle and physical agility.

In the 1870s, a strong trend towards competitive athletics settled in on American campuses. However, resistance still existed. When the University of Michigan challenged Cornell to a football game (1873), President Andrew White telegraphed back that he would not "permit thirty men to travel four hundred miles merely to agitate a bag of wind." Other presidents, however, realized early what value sports had for publicity. After winning the Sarasota regatta, Columbia president Barnard proudly proclaimed (1874) that "little was known about Columbia one month ago, but today wherever the telegraph cable extends, the existence of Columbia College is known and respected." After Cornell's varsity and frosh crews won the same regatta (1875), its president wired both crews, "The University chimes are ringing, flags flying and cannons firing," and he absorbed the then enormous debt of $1,100 the crews had incurred and wrote it off as advertising. Harvard's president, Charles W. Eliot, who had rowed crew as an undergraduate, later became disenchanted with the dominating influence of athletics on his campus and tried hard to keep education in perspective. Nevertheless, he awarded a full Harvard scholarship to a C-student, "Home Run" Franz, who was reputed to be the greatest college first baseman of his time.

Other college presidents engaged themselves fully in their schools' sports. The presidents of Trinity College, now Duke University, and Miami of Ohio established football teams as a means of making their schools better known. President Crowell even coached the Trinity squad—possibly the only president-football coach ever in American higher education. Vernon Parrington joined the English Department at the University of Oklahoma and, remaining a professor, became the football coach before he rose to the school's presidency (1897). The prize though goes to President Warfield who played on his own school's football team (1888) and insisted that all able-bodied men at Miami of Ohio play on the team. He was seriously injured during team practice one day. I suspect a short story is buried here. Had the president recently established an unpopular student policy? Was this a unique chance for a recently disciplined student to get back at his president? There is limitless room for speculation.

As long as professors or even a president doubled as coaches, commercialization of college athletics was held at bay. But soon came the professional coaches, and big money entered the picture. Yale's athletic budget climbed from $18,000 in 1880 to $50,000 in the 1890s, until its football income alone (1903) was greater than the combined income of Yale's law, divinity, and medical schools ($106,000). President Warfield of Lafayette College, then a rising football power, stated that one Thanksgiving game brought in revenue exceeding the college's total annual academic budget (1905). Soon after, serious discussions about reforms in college sports began. They have been going on ever since. So far the only major change seems to be that presidents have stopped coaching and playing on their own teams.

May 1, 2002

∾

Thinking of Robert Frost on a sunny day in Chicago

I was sitting in a sidewalk café in Chicago, enjoying my caffè latte, taking in the sunshine, and observing the energizing hustle of the windy city when an old van pulled up to the curb and spilled out several young men and women with long hair, headbands, jeans, and colorful clothing. They immediately began unloading musical instruments, synthesizers, guitars, a huge percussion set, heavy amplifiers—and placing them carefully on the curb and then carrying the whole heavy load into the building. Obviously, a poor and young band of musicians was setting up for a gig. I could read it in the faces of all the latte drinkers around me: I am glad these are not my kids.

The night before I had done my own gig, speaking in an elegant hotel at an alumni meeting. After a cocktail reception, well-trained waiters had served a delicious meal during which expensively dressed young men and women had renewed acquaintances, networked, and exchanged calling cards and inside information about their workplaces. Cell phones were in evidence all over, dangling from belts and purses, ready to receive calls while drinks and meals were served and speakers introduced. A different group of young people at work and play, well attuned to market trends, the 'in' restaurants, and the latest fashions. All of them dear to me, bright, pleasant, ambitious, self-confident, and 'on the way up.' Each one of them a tuition-paying parent's dream come true.

A greater contrast was hard to imagine. A group of young urban professionals inside a fine hotel and a young band of musicians out at the curbside—both pursuing their dreams and doing what they do best. As I compared them, I saw before me the thousands of students who had passed through my classes and my office, all so very likeable, so promising, and yet each so different in talent, aspirations, and choices. Now I met them again, no longer college students, but working professionals receiving their guidance from bosses and colleagues at work. Young people learning new lessons: how to compromise, how to blend into existing corporate cultures, how to please superiors or customers, and how to advance. And then those others, at the curbside of life, who do not quite fit in but elect to spend their lives as musicians, actors, painters, or writers, with very little chance to ever reap riches or to exercise stock options.

Parents are mindful of the varying rewards that youthful life and career choices bring. I recall the father who stopped tuition payments when his daughter switched her major from engineering to philosophy. I have observed terror in the eyes of parents whose son declared that he wanted to be an actor rather than finish dental school. I have often talked for hours with students who were considering changing their majors in midstream.

And always my heart has been with those who chose the difficult path. I love all students, regardless of their chosen profession. Of course, we need devoted and competent engineers and accountants. But they usually find their spots easily, and life rewards them appropriately. Not so in the arts. No student who risks becoming an actor, a painter, or a writer ever believes that this is going to be an easy road. They all sense that after years of hard and dedicated work they may meet with mainly disappointment and rejection. And yet they march courageously ahead, full of hope, and driven by their dreams. I always felt that students in the arts and humanities needed my particular protection and support. I envy them their beautiful dreams. And I admire their enormous courage. I embrace them in my heart as one embraces those daring to go into battle in which only few shall find victory.

As I finished my caffè latte, I watched the musicians go on with their arduous work. I watched them with kinship and admiration, and my heart greeted them on their road less traveled by. Indeed, their choices do make all the difference.

June 14, 2000

∾

Utopian hopes for young people today

When I advised the trustees of our university that I intended to return to the faculty after a long tenure in administration, I did not use the fairly standard cliché that I was returning to teaching, my first love. I had taught with enthusiasm for many years in my early career and continued to teach occasionally while I was provost and president. But my first love was actually research, not teaching. The prospect of making a living by asking interesting questions and being engaged in continual intellectual inquiry was what attracted me originally to university life.

Once in awhile, however, teaching and intellectual curiosity, the causes for all research, join to form a union. I experienced such a moment during the semester I scheduled a course on

"Utopian Societies from Antiquity to our Times." I intended to explain and interpret for my students texts composed by philosophers, writers, and social reformers during the last two thousand years—such as Plato's *Republic, Utopia* by Thomas More, *The American Declaration of Independence* and the *U.S. Constitution, The Communist Manifesto,* Edward Bellamy's *Looking Backward,* Aldous Huxley's *Brave New World*, George Orwell's *Animal Farm,* and others. I was ready to lecture about the many attempts in America to build ideal societies by social reformers such as Robert Owen or religious groups such as the Shakers. It could have become a course of interesting lectures, but my students surprised me by taking charge of the class. Instead of settling for a string of lectures, we engaged in serious discussion and debate throughout the semester. I have seldom so enjoyed an intellectual involvement with a group of students.

Certain miracles occurred, and other teachers will quickly recognize them. First, except for a severe illness, there were no absences. Second, students came to class prepared. The assigned texts had been read, and carefully written essays had been prepared. All of them on time, none of them eaten by the dog the night before, or delayed because of a breakdown of the printer—two frequently heard excuses. Third, a few times we exceeded the scheduled class time—two and a half long hours—and I, the teacher, had to stop the discussion. Every student contributed. It was a teacher's dream come true.

And we delved into all the questions that men and women, at least once in their lives, should think about deeply. Why have thinkers since time immemorial philosophized about how an ideal society should be constituted? Which are the ideals that great thinkers considered basic to social justice? Was it liberty, individualism or the common good, religious faith, altruism, tolerance, the pursuit of happiness, or a classless society? What do all these values mean in our society and in our personal lives? And on the other hand: what problems have social reformers identified as the most divisive and most destructive in a society? Is it poverty and unequal distribution of wealth, lack of equality, oppression, or caste systems? What qualities should those possess who rule over others? Should they be philosopher-kings who are wise, courageous, and immune to the temptations of power?

At the end of the semester, three student groups designed their own ideal societies which reflected the team members' ideas about fair and workable social and political systems, about race and gender equality, marriage and family, public education, and healthcare. Our long discussions about these questions had born fruit. The student presentations demonstrated not only intelligence and imagination, but I was actually moved by my students' lofty degree of social responsibility, their sense of fairness, and moral character. We so often complain in our town about students—their drinking, their rowdiness, their lack of respect. I wish our community could have sat next to these twenty students from the Lee Honors College. Any outsider would have been impressed, as I was, with these truly fine, smart, witty, responsible, and caring youngsters whose ability, intelligence, and social conscience guarantee that our future is in the best of hands. The semester boosted my optimism about young people enormously. I am sorry the course is over.

December 11, 2002

≈

California sets college admissions trends

Californians are trendsetters in food, fashion, and lifestyle, but now they also lead the avant-garde in education. In 1996, California voters passed Proposition 209, which banned the use of race in hiring and admissions. The usual cries of racial discrimination were hurled around—and the defenders of racial quotas (or goals, or critical masses) in college admissions issued firm predictions that the implementation of the ban would devastate the number of minority students on California campuses. Without racial preferences, they argued, Blacks and Hispanics simply would not be able to compete with white students.

However, the doomsayers of higher education were wrong in their prophecies of woe. Minority enrollment on the undergraduate campuses of the University of California was 18% in 1997, the last year that racial preferences in admissions were applied.

In 2001, with race no longer an admissions criterion, that figure topped 19%. Granted, minority presence on the two most prestigious campuses, Berkeley and Los Angeles, fell, and the minority students are now more evenly distributed among the other system campuses, where presumably they will be more competitive, have stronger success experiences, better grades, and higher graduation rates. This is exactly what everyone should want, and the measures taken should be considered a success. It also proves that minority students can indeed meet the standards of higher education, which should be a great source of confidence and respect. I predict that in due course, minority numbers on the Berkeley and Los Angeles campuses will again reach their previous levels. Eventually, nobody will be able to remark condescendingly that minority students on those campuses attend because of preferential treatment.

But the education establishment cannot leave well enough alone. Recently, the president of the University of California system called for the elimination of the widely used SAT test as an admissions requirement. While this test is a very reliable predictor of academic achievement and of success in the freshman year, many consider it biased against Blacks. For at least two decades, black educators have been asked to identify the test's areas of bias, and all objectionable points were eliminated, but the result is still the same: Blacks, as a group, do not perform as well on the SAT as Whites. Hence the claim of bias.

Shackled by the voters' ban on racial preferences and the threat of judicial interference, the California university regents recently adopted a policy that de-emphasizes the objectivity of the SAT and adds the "personal record" of the student as an admissions consideration. Has the student overcome poverty, hardship, family problems, handicaps, or personal challenges? These are the new questions weighed in the "holistic" admissions process.

In satirical letters, Californian parents have pondered if they should start drinking heavily, beating up their kids occasionally, or divorcing their spouses in order to provide the hardship experiences their children now need for entrance into the state's best public universities. Being a bright, well-loved, two-parent kid growing up in a safe neighborhood could henceforth be a hazard to chances for admission.

I worry more about another problem. Smart students know how to finesse the system. Application letters, already largely co-authored by a committee of student, parent, expert friends, and counselors will rise to a new art form. Who will check out all the imaginative claims of hardship prospective students will make in their application letters? Will colleges send out detectives to verify wife beatings, parental drinking problems, prison records of siblings, and claims of negative peer pressure? Or will the recommendations written by social workers henceforth outweigh those produced by academic teachers and advisors? And further: a comprehensive "holistic" evaluation should take at the very least one half hour. If a campus receives 15,000 to 20,000 applications to be screened by an admissions committee of at least 3 people, 60,000 hours or 60 administrators or faculty would have to work full-time for half a year to do the job. Who believes that this will really happen? What will happen instead is that with highly subjective instead of objective admissions standards, the University of California can finally, without court or voter interference, admit whomever they want. So much for the courts and the voters!

September 4, 2002

∼

Each semester brings highs and lows

It is Final Exam week on campus. Waldo Library currently sees more students than at any other time during the semester, their heads bowed over notes and books, yellow markers in hand, underlining anything in sight. Cramming is the last crucial mile of the academic long-distance run.

Waldo's Campus Tavern is also crammed, as I observed last night. Here assemble those delighted souls whose exams lie behind them or those less happy students who forego cramming and instead, bent over a beer, pin their hopes on good luck, merciful teachers, and hopeful prayer.

I am done. The academic year is over with. I gave my final exams, handed in my class grades, and now I only have to deal with the deeply disappointed students whose prayers for divine intervention and miraculous results on their tests went unanswered. Time to celebrate and to reflect.

Each semester opens with great enthusiasm on my side. I am excited about what I will teach. I look forward to knowing each student in my class, and I am eager to give all of them the instruction, the patience, and the assistance needed for effective learning. I hope each one of them will enjoy the class, and I want each one to succeed. In all this I am just like any teacher at the beginning of a course.

And then follow all the high and low moments of the semester. The highs are luckily more frequent than the lows. College students, by and large, are bright, eager to learn, respectful, quite tolerant of others, often very generous to their classmates, usually very practical; and it is a great pleasure, a privilege even, to be their teacher. The ultimate high is to see how a younger mind gets interested in a new concept, in new knowledge, and begins to pursue it with excitement or even passion. Each teacher sees a reflection of himself in that student and remembers his own initial fascination with a particular subject that often became central to his life. I feel elated when I can bring a student to see a seemingly familiar fact in a new light, or when I can make students read a text with which they are already acquainted with new eyes and changed insight. Similarly, to see students acquire and eventually master skills under my tutelage is a highly rewarding moment. At moments like those I am grateful to be a member of the world's second oldest profession.

But there are also the other, less happy, moments each semester. Spotting early on the student who does not apply himself properly; who does not respond to admonition and ample offers of assistance and good advice; and who will predictably become an academic casualty. Too few students ever make good use of their professors' office hours. One sits and waits for those who need help, but they will only appear moments before the final exam when missed class time and broad gaps in reading and learning make any rescue mission hopeless. If only one could convince students that professors are not fire departments to be called upon when the house is already engulfed in flame. Entering the final D or E on the grade sheet is a painful and dreaded duty. Wasted effort and unfulfilled potential always depress me to no end.

But at the end of each semester, as soon as the unavoidable sigh of relief is breathed, one begins to look forward to the next fall with its new exciting courses and with new ideas on how to improve last year's classes. And each fall brings a new crop of students. Already the future freshmen are scurrying about campus, during orientation visits with their parents, and I look at them and wonder if any of them will sit in front of me in the fall. I am certainly ready for them.

April 26, 2000

~

Keep graduation speeches short and beautiful

Each spring heralds the time for commencement exercises in schools and colleges all over the country. Students usually have their eyes riveted on the future while they bid farewell to classmates and friends. Parents, however, have their thoughts more likely focused on the past. During the graduation ceremonies that I attended as a father, my own thoughts were wandering backwards, not forwards. I remembered the days my little girl and boy were born, how they had sat on my lap when I read them their first stories, their first days in school, the trips we had taken together, and how they had grown up, quite imperceptibly, into independence and selfhood. Having presided over countless university commencements, I held very different feelings while seeing my own children receive the official handshake and diploma. And while I was sitting there with thousands of people, surrounded by all the pomp and circumstance of the festive ceremonies, I harbored my own very private thoughts, clutching the hand of my wife at whose side this amazingly quick, and yet so lengthy journey from pre-school to college had been traveled. Like all other parents I felt overcome with joy and pride, awash in emotion, and deeply grateful for all the glorious, tender, and unforgettable moments with which my children's lives had enriched mine.

All parents come to the ceremony essentially in order to see their son or daughter cross the stage and to share the high moment of accomplishment and success that is reached on that day. I am convinced that very few parents listen attentively to the commencement address, and I must admit that even my mind drifted away to more personal thoughts at my children's graduation. However, when I shared the stage with the speakers, I had to listen more carefully because they usually expected some laudatory comments afterwards over lunch. Thus I have listened to literally hundreds of commencement speeches, among them one endless discourse on the financial markets in Southeast Asia, which brought the students to the edge of rebellion. I have also heard an American president make a major policy speech; I have listened to famous authors shamelessly promoting their books; and I have endured an unintelligible speech by a foreign diplomat which left the audience divided in its opinion on whether the speech was delivered in English or Hungarian. When I became president, I persuaded our trustees to do away with formal commencement speeches. Although I have no quantifiable evidence, I believe student attendance at our WMU ceremony rose steadily from that moment on.

Most schools, however, continue the tradition of the formal commencement speaker. I myself was frequently asked to speak at other institutions' graduation ceremonies, but I was invited because my fellow presidents knew I habitually stuck to three basic pieces of knowledge. I always remembered that on graduation day nobody ever wants to listen to another academic lecture. I had also learned over time that nobody ever complains about a commencement speech being too short. And from my own experience I knew that hardly any graduate ever remembers what wisdom exactly had been dispensed, thirty years earlier, by the commencement speaker. With this in mind, I kept my own addresses very brief, light, and humorous, and saved the customary deep and ponderous academic thoughts for another day.

Many years ago, at another university, we decided to bestow

an honorary degree on Marian Anderson, the famous contralto who once (1939) had been barred, because of her race, from concertizing in Constitution Hall, and who later (1955) became the first black singer to perform at the Metropolitan Opera. Her concert career already lay behind her when we met. She had been asked to speak to the graduates, and everyone expected her to dwell on the many racial barriers she had to overcome in her life. She stepped to the microphone and looked for a long time into the young faces of our students who watched her in rapt anticipation. Slowly she put her speech notes aside, and then she sang "America, the Beautiful." I doubt anyone present that day will ever forget Marian Anderson's commencement speech.

June 26, 2002

∼

Can great art be insensitive?

While I was WMU president, I truly loved my job. Now, when I read of reduced budget allocations, tuition increases, or student protests, I smile with relief and am pleased that these problems will never cross my desk again.

But with each such report, a sense of *déjà vu* overcomes me. After 25 years in university administration, there are few topics I haven't dealt with before, and before, and before. And no matter how often one thinks they are resolved, they return every few years with each new student generation. One of the ever-recurring topics is the vague concept of 'insensitivity.'

Many of today's students hold that anything they consider discomforting, unwelcoming, or offensive shows the 'insensitivity' of their professors, their fellow students, or even the entire institution. Terms such as unwelcoming, discomforting, or insensitive are rather ambiguous, and very few students are willing or able to give a thoughtful and clear definition of any of them. Their definitions are as opaque and vague as their accusations.

Students often fail to accept that in the course of all rigorous and honest education, and particularly in an environment in which free speech and academic freedom are guaranteed, one comes, by definition, in contact with ideas, facts, or artistic creations that may appear overwhelming, upsetting, and even revolting. Students should not enter a university with the expectation that their belief system will not be challenged, and that their viewpoints will not be tested and held up for comparison. Too many students have been raised to believe that their inchoate feelings and opinions are just as valuable as the hard knowledge of those who are appointed to teach them.

A case in point. In 1930, the prominent painter Thomas Hart Benton was commissioned by the public arts program during the Depression to create 26 very large murals depicting the social and industrial history of the state of Indiana. The artist decided to paint that history, warts and all. For that reason, one of the panels depicts in the background a burning cross and Klan members. In the twenties, the Klan exercised strong political power in Indiana, opposing immigration, Catholics, Jews, Blacks, and the perceived moral decay of America. The murals are installed at Indiana University. Indiana history professor James Madison thinks that in order to understand Indiana, one has to understand what role the Klan played in its history. The depiction of the American flag and a church in the painting indicate the Klan's roots in local militant patriotism and religious fundamentalism. Images of the press, in the foreground of the picture, indicate that the Klan was exposed and eventually overcome by a free press. Professor Madison considers the mural an important statement on the dark underside of his state's history that must be taught. "We need to face our past and our present," he says. "This is a university, and our purpose is to help students see things and understand what that mural is."

But the political action chairwoman of the Black Student Union sees only the Klan images and not the story the mural tries to tell. She feels intimidated by the painting, which she perceives as insensitive and as providing an unwelcome environment. Her demand: the mural should either be removed or no classes should be offered in the lecture hall.

African-American students and the administration have met repeatedly. The professors tried to teach the students that the painting illustrates the victory of the press over ignorance and hate and therefore serves an important educational purpose. Still, the Black Student Union declares the images of the Klan in the painting "offending" and wants it removed and replaced by images from the Civil Rights movement. "We are speaking to deaf ears," say the students whose own ears are deaf to what their professors try to teach them.

The murals, considered national treasures, cannot be moved without damage. I hope they will stay as they are. If they were replaced or destroyed, the teaching of history in one of our great universities would take a backseat to providing a 'welcoming environment.' In that environment, everyone will lose.

March 13, 2002

∼

Campus brochures: let the buyer beware

As college acceptance letters arrive, graduating high school seniors must decide which school to attend. Most of them make multiple applications, and everyone who gets into Harvard, Stanford, or MIT and has the cash needed for those high-priced schools won't hesitate to move without further soul searching into these penthouses of higher education. But if the invitation is only for a lower floor or even the basement in the tower of learning, the family digs out last year's recruitment brochures and reconsiders.

Most students claim to select their universities because of academic quality. They tell us this because they know it is what professors want to hear. But I have always been suspicious of that statement. For perhaps one quarter of all students it may be true. The other three quarters, I suspect, are guided by other and not necessarily inappropriate considerations. Where do my best friends go? Who offers me the best financial aid/scholarship deal? How far away from home/my girlfriend/my boyfriend is this school? Is it a 'fun' campus? Does it have winning sports teams? What do the sophomores and juniors I know on the campus say about the school?

Perhaps these criteria are not altogether unsuitable for many students when making a college choice. In any case, current students may be more honest than some of the brochures colleges mail to prospective students. Recruitment brochures, expensive and beautiful, are as reliable as any glossy sales offer one receives from someone who wants to sell a product. They only accentuate the positive, as the song goes, and leave the negative unsaid.

Every page of a college recruitment brochure usually shows the faces of deliriously happy students engaged in sports, homecoming activities, or doughnut eating contests. When not engaged in leisure activities, the students are active in musical and theatrical events, or sit in the campus library, bent over books, deeply absorbed. (No pictures ever of students glued to soaps on TV.) Needless to say, in the brochures all students wear T-shirts or baseball caps with the school's name on them. (I, however, remember students wearing MSU sweatshirts while sitting at our reception desk welcoming campus visitors.)

Brochures always show the campus during the spring or autumn—tulips in bloom or maples in splendid colors. The buildings, including efficient classrooms, well-equipped labs, and cheerful dormitory rooms, all look as if they were built yesterday and as if eager cleaning crews swept through them every other hour.

Another striking observation is that all these campuses have a perfect gender and racial mix. No recruitment brochure will show three white males studying together, not even in the engineering school, or three African-American women sitting together at lunch in the cafeteria. No, that comes too close to reality and won't be shown for the same reason that it never rains in any of the pictures. Miraculously, owing to years of wishful PC thinking, our catalogs show all student groups perfectly mixed by race and gender, Asians frolicking with Latinos, white folk with black students. If such photos of racial harmony do not exist in the photo archives of a school, they can be doctored with photo-design software, as was recently discovered in catalogs of the University of Wisconsin and the University of Idaho where two white students were digitally decapitated and two new faces—one Asian, one black—pasted on their white bodies.

I remember once attempting to get capital outlay funds by lamenting the sad state of our campus in the governor's office. In response, the governor simply put my university's latest recruitment brochure in front of me. It displayed modern buildings studded with state-of-the-art labs surrounded by manicured lawns and swans cruising on a lovely pond. A wealthy country club could not have looked more inviting. I had shot down my argument with my own brochure.

Glossy college catalogs are sales brochures. Nobody buys a car from a catalog. When buying a car, ask other owners how they like it. Take it out for a spin, and find out for yourself. The same, it seems, goes for colleges.

February 27, 2002

∽

Thoughts at the beginning of the college sports season

A few years ago a colleague and I met, at a hotel checkout desk in Dallas, the presidents of Central and Eastern Michigan universities, and the four of us decided to share the cost of transportation to the airport. We piled into a hot and narrow taxi. As we were unloading our luggage at the curbside check-in, a chauffeur-driven limousine pulled up and out stepped the Athletic Director of the University of Michigan who had attended the same NCAA conference. We saw him later sipping a beverage in his first class seat as three Michigan university presidents passed him on their way into steerage. It was a symbolic moment: academics meets athletics. We had a good laugh about it at the time, but we also thought that a few things in some big athletics programs were perhaps out of kilter.

When I worked as chief academic officer in a Big 10 school, we divided universities into those where most students knew the name of the president (usually a distinguished professor) and those universities where most students knew the name of the football coach but not that of their president or any academic dean. Not many big schools made it into the first category. I believe this situation was typical for the entire Big 10 and very likely still

36

prevails today in most schools with top-ranked athletics programs.

What has happened in our universities? Is the tail wagging the dog? There is no doubt: while most of our national public universities are academic jewels and the envy of the world, most Americans know these schools for their athletic prowess, their athletic teams' presence on TV, and their appearances in the mushrooming bowl games.

I mused with Chris Reynolds, an assistant athletic director, about these questions. He knows the big time having played basketball at Indiana for one of the game's most legendary coaches. (I probably don't have to name that coach, but does anyone know who is president of Indiana University?) Mr. Reynolds thinks that the year 1993 was one of the big turning points in college sports when the NCAA negotiated a $1 Billion contract with CBS, which gave the network exclusive rights to the basketball tournaments for several years.

At that time big money entered college sports, and administrators realized how much revenue could be created with college athletics. Every Division I conference in the land began to lust after TV contracts, and the institutional coffers filled up. Many universities charge ticket prices that are almost out of reach for normal wage earners. Yet there are always more than enough fans who want to see the big games. And price seems to be no object. Ask anyone who ever scalped tickets for, let's say, a U of M vs. Notre Dame football game.

College athletics has become big business. Americans love sports, and their appetite for them seems insatiable. And the universities are cashing in on the sports mania. The enormous revenues from TV and from contracts with manufacturers of sports equipment, combined with the income from school logos, concessions, and parking bring unprecedented wealth.

An anecdote from Ohio State football history illuminates probably the last time when academics attempted to control the growing influence of sports in their university. In 1961, undefeated in the Big 10 and having trounced Michigan 50-20, OSU was scheduled to go to the Rose Bowl. However, the Faculty Council, fearing that the academic reputation of the school was being overshadowed by the enormous popularity of coach Woody

Hayes' football program, voted not to send his team to the Rose Bowl. Open warfare ensued on campus and all over the state of Ohio. But the faculty prevailed, and the Big Ten champion did not go to Pasadena that year.

Today it is inconceivable that such a vote would ever be taken or, if taken, that it would stand. Big money and sports mania rule athletics, and Don Quixote tilted his last windmill long ago.

September 8, 1999

~

Teaching devotion, courage, and leadership

A few weeks ago, a judge in Montana called me to renew acquaintance. She had seen my name somewhere and decided to tell me that thirty years ago she had sat in my Goethe seminar in Detroit. I did not remember her, but she recalled in detail concepts we discussed way back then that had stuck with her to this day. I was glad and mightily pleased to be thus remembered. Obviously, I am not without vanity.

Teachers in the humanities can seldom assess the effect and the longevity of what they teach. That's why I derive such great satisfaction from teaching German to freshmen. After a few weeks we can exchange greetings, express simple desires, and ask inelaborate questions. Our joint efforts quickly show tangible results: we can communicate in basic ways in a new idiom. However, what if one conducts seminars on literary works or historical figures? At the end of such courses, who can determine how much has been learned, what exactly has been learned, and how much of it will stick with the learner beyond the final exam? Will any one of my current students remember in thirty years what we discussed during this semester? I will never find out because I don't expect to answer the telephone at that time.

This semester we studied the life of Joan of Arc (1412-1431), a country girl from Lorraine, who rose from total obscurity in one of France's darkest hours to command the French army, inspiring the demoralized troops to victory against the occupying English.

38

In a short, glorious military campaign she lifted not only the siege of Orléans, but triumphantly conquered several cities on her way to Reims. There she saw the hapless dauphin crowned King of France, just as she claimed her heavenly voices had told her she would. A year later, betrayed by her king, captured by the Burgundians, and sold to the English, she was burned as a heretic after a lengthy trial conducted by the same Catholic Church that canonized her five hundred years later.

The Maiden, as she was called at the time, stepped into the full light of history for only two years (1429-1431) but has inspired the literary imagination more than practically any other historical figure. Tchaikovsky and Verdi, among others, wrote operas about her. German, French, Italian, English, and American writers chose her as a literary subject. Many movies were made about Joan of Arc, and I had the pleasure to examine with a large group of bright honors students the many different ways the artistic imagination has interpreted this unusual woman.

Who was she? Was she the witch the English wanted to burn? Or a pious, simple girl following the commands given by St. Michael and St. Catherine? Was she a heretic claiming to have direct, personal contact with God, rejecting the Church as an intermediary? Or was she a brilliant military leader, a natural talent in warfare, and the last great knight of the Middle Ages? Or an anorexic cross-dressing teenager, centuries ahead of her times? Was she a messenger of God, or an imposter skillfully using contemporary superstitions to her advantage?

As is often the case in the humanities, we did not arrive at definitive answers, but at possibilities. Evidence was examined, personal beliefs tested, religious, psychological, historical, artistic aspects contemplated. The best a teacher may expect is that his students for a semester think deeply about a historical phenomenon that, in the last analysis, must remain an enigma.

However, convention demands that each student receive a grade, and so I must concoct a final exam. My students will have to identify figures such as Pièrre Cauchon, Henry VI, and the Bastard of Orléans. They must write essays on the Holy Inquisition, on Jean Anouilh's dramatic technique, the Battle of Agincourt, or on Mark Twain's St. Joan novel. This sort of knowledge will determine the students' final grade. But actually

I hope that a few of them might rather remember our discussions of the possibility of faithful devotion, heroic courage, and the power of inspired leadership. Something that might still be in their memories thirty years from now.

December 5, 2001

∼

A (not so serious) proposal
for an academic classification system

Ever since I became a university department chairman, I have pondered the blandness of the academic classification system. Could it be made more descriptive?

Everyone who ever went to college knows that professors come in untold different varieties and flavors, but there are only three banal sounding ranks: assistant, associate, and full professor. That does not do the existing idiosyncratic variety any justice, and a future column must deal with an innovative classification system for professors. I am open to suggestions.

This time I want to deal with department chairs, formerly called chairmen and even earlier called department heads. Their quality is essential to any well-run university.

When I became a full professor after nine years of toiling in the academic vineyards, I had also been a department chair for some time. I loved being a department chair. It is the best job and the worst job in the university. There is the direct daily intellectual contact with students and faculty, and the most important issues in the university—namely teaching and research—take place on this level.

But to be chair also means holding the tough front line in the university with all the daily drudgery. The chair's office is the student complaint department; the faculty complaint department; the counseling couch for all departmental prima donnas; the accountability department for the higher administration; and the advocate general's office representing the faculty against the, by definition, ever capricious and malevolent administration.

Ever since I held that job, I have been convinced that it is one of the most important positions in the university. Over the years, whenever I had to select chairs, I exercised special care and developed my own classification system for the men and women whom I appointed.

Most appealing to me has always been the 'straight chair' who tells it like it is. Such chairs give you clear answers and are good for their word. They operate in sharp contrast to the 'rocking chairs,' who go back and forth in their opinions on practically all matters of consequence.

The 'lounge chair' spends most of his or her time at the faculty club and is seldom found in the department. I have known a few who turned into 'bar stools' if their prolonged absences were caused by other than academic habits. Many departments are happy with an 'occasional chair' who chairs only intermittently and only when it does not matter.

The 'recliner' is loved by many faculty because he or she will bend over if tipped ever so slightly, and 'recliners' remain in that position until someone behind them straightens their spines by bringing them back into an upright position. The 'recliner' is, administratively speaking, a close cousin to the 'folding chair' who is put to use only on special occasions and can be collapsed and removed easily to be put into storage until needed again. Subcategories of the 'recliner' are the 'footstool' whose function is to be stepped upon; and the 'potty chair' who is usually full of what needs no explanation and definition.

The moniker 'high chair' belongs to those over 6'3", whereas 'antique chair' refers to all who have held that position longer than fifteen years.

This more descriptive classification system has served me well in my days. I claim no copyright or patent to it and offer it to any organization that wishes to adopt it.

What kind of chair was I when I served in that position? I'd like to leave that to the judgment of my academic colleagues, but 'recliner' and 'footstool' I was not. 'Easy chair' might come closest, if that means someone who refuses to take things too seriously, is not too formal, and is thoroughly comfortable with his role.

September 22, 1999

⁓

Grade inflation at Harvard—and elsewhere

If my neighbor had come over a year ago to tell me that his son was graduated from Harvard with honors, I would have been quite thrilled. Today, a year later, the same accomplishment impresses me much less. To the embarrassment of the university's administration, the *Boston Globe* revealed that practically everyone at Harvard graduated with honors—91% of all students, to be exact. Is the picture similar at Yale and Princeton? Not quite, although even at these about every second student graduates *cum laude* or better.

Earlier last year, a Harvard professor, resentful of the lax grading practices of his colleagues, had informed his students that he would henceforth give them two grades. One grade to be entered onto their transcript, and a second one that would reflect his honest, professional assessment of their academic accomplishment. The professor felt that if he graded appropriately, his accurate evaluations would negatively affect the grade point averages of his students. They would, in other words, receive lower grades than their classmates who attended his colleagues' classes in which 51% of all students typically receive A's and A-'s for their work. But he felt strongly that his students had to be given an honest opinion of the actual level of their academic achievement in the subject matter he taught; thus the second, honest grade, which would not appear on their records.

The revelation that A's are that easy to get at Harvard, sent shock waves through the corridors of higher education. It shouldn't have. Grade inflation is rampant throughout the academy, and every professor knows it. To many of today's students, a C is an almost unacceptable grade. Having given a student a C/B last semester, I received an enraged letter from her. "I do not believe that I should have received a grade any lower than B/A," she wrote and pointed to the fact that, "I have never spent more time and effort on a paper in my entire life." This may be true, but I don't give an A for effort. "If the final exam was the part that lowered the grade," she continued, "it is ridiculous." Yes, her final exam was very poor, and with an old-fashioned professor such as

I this fact influences the final grade, ridiculous as it may seem. "I wish you to examine my paper and my exam again and re-evaluate my grade," she concluded her indignant missive.

To those who were graduated twenty years ago, the tone of this letter and its argumentation must seem—to say the least—bold. I certainly can't imagine having attempted a similar exchange with my professors when I was a student. Things do change though. There is generally less readiness for rigor in academic work. Evaluations of professors by students are commonplace, and hard graders get less favorable assessments. One of many other reasons may be that the modern university is increasingly run like a corporation in which administrators tell students that they are 'consumers' and 'paying customers' who may expect excellent service. I agree only with the spirit of the latter part of this statement. Yes, the student should receive excellent service, and that means to me that there should be a well-trained, highly informed, and competent teacher; a tolerant, harassment-free classroom; and a general environment conducive to learning. However, when it comes to assessing the students' accomplishments, there can be no haggling as in the market place, and the more experienced, more knowledgeable teacher assesses the relative accomplishment of the learner. It can't be any other way.

But it is often easier to simply assign an A or an A- and avoid the hassle. It makes the student happy, the parents content, and saves the teacher a lot of work. However, it leads to questionable standards and, as the Harvard case has shown, to public embarrassment. Granted, Harvard students are carefully selected and very bright, but if 91% are graduating with honors, the honors designation becomes meaningless, and something is wrong. But it is not just wrong at Harvard. We should all learn a lesson from this.

January 16, 2002

≈

Let's not run universities like businesses

American universities are highly complex enterprises. When I left Ohio State in 1985, the university had 17,000 employees and, at that time, already an annual budget exceeding $1 Billion. It is significantly higher today. With close to 60,000 students distributed over 19 schools and colleges, giant residence halls, food services for tens of thousands of daily customers, major hospitals, numerous farms, enormous athletic facilities, a vast extension service, and research labs throughout the state, the university could also be regarded as a major economic power and one of the region's dominant businesses.

And, indeed, by many it was seen that way. The trustees, most of them businessmen, often appeared slightly uneasy when they realized that the people administering this enormous enterprise did not come from business backgrounds but had spent many years of their lives studying soil erosion in Africa, treating diseases of the eye, or teaching courses in contemporary poetry. That included me, and the suspicion of incompetence shrouded me like all others who had not earned their spurs in finance, marketing, or sales.

To alleviate our trustees' concerns, we attempted to familiarize university management with contemporary business practices, many of which turned out to be short-lived fads. I don't know how many lectures on the then highly touted Japanese business practices I attended before that business world committed financial seppuku. Then we were taught by guru Deming to exceed the customer's expectations and to do things right the first time—the latter of which is hard to do if one works in the area of experimentation and research. We learned about zero-based budgeting, just-on-time delivery, quality circles, employee empowerment, and, quite honestly, many of these concepts proved applicable and helpful for the purely business aspects of the university: purchasing, construction, plant maintenance, food services, and the like.

However, none of these techniques proved to be a general prescription for running a university. They are germane only to one, and not the most important aspect of a university. The concept that institutions of higher learning are like businesses fails to recognize that universities, museums or symphonies, and hospitals are not primarily businesses—although they all need to generate money, must advertise, and manage personnel. But their *raison d'être* is different. They do not aim at selling a product with which to make a profit. They create knowledge, esthetic enjoyment, or facilitate healing. Their very core purpose is thus essentially different from any business.

The business aspects of universities, complex as they admittedly are, can be learned by intelligent people reasonably quickly and easily. The British ran their vast empire with people who had read Latin or history at Oxford and Cambridge before they entered the civil service or the management of world-wide companies. I learned labor relations at the knee of a former union negotiator of American Motors, and a former partner of Ernst & Young taught me how to read balance sheets as well as how to find and how to hide money. Both were at the time university executives. But conversely, it is much more difficult for businessmen to comprehend the core values of a university and to become comfortable with its elaborate and Gordian governance structure.

Compared with what has happened in the business world in recent years, universities are, by and large, exceptionally well run. They don't go bankrupt, and if they would, they certainly would not pay their presidents millions of dollars in severance pay after two years of service, as K-Mart did. They don't know mass lay-offs. They don't merge with other universities, making their top executives rich and leaving many employees out in the street. Their market value does not rise and sink from one month to the next. They don't move their headquarters from city to city.

People who insist that universities have much to learn from businesses and should act more businesslike, should think of Enron, the Keating Five, the dot.com companies, Arthur Andersen, or K-Mart, and then reconsider if the people who manage universities while reading 19th century novels or playing cello are really doing so poorly.

March 20, 2002

∼

45

Parents should set responsible example in the use of alcohol

When I was still smoking and my doctor asked me about my daily cigarette consumption, I rarely answered truthfully. But Dr. McKeever knew that. He told me that he routinely doubled the number the patient admitted.

Once, after being interviewed by a student newspaper about alcohol abuse on American campuses, I asked the young reporter how much, if any, alcohol he personally consumed, and would he consider himself a heavy drinker. No, he assured me cheerfully, he was strictly a social drinker, no more than perhaps a six-pack per night. I thought of Dr. McKeever's formula and realized that the young man had a serious problem.

We regularly hear of fatalities on some of the nation's best-known campuses, stunning events in which students literally drink themselves to death. College administrators have reacted with alarm, but can essentially do very little. Beer advertisements in college publications have been banned; tailgating with alcohol has been curtailed or outlawed; "substance free zones" have been created in residence halls; and fraternities have vowed to make their houses and rushes alcohol free.

Will it help? One certainly hopes so. After all, besides the deaths that raised the national consciousness, we know that most date rapes occur under the influence of alcohol; and most vandalism, most violence, most traffic accidents among students stand in direct relationship to alcohol consumption.

The most dangerous and least fathomable habit is the widely observed binge drinking. Students who during the week might not drink at all, begin the weekend (which often begins Thursday night) with the clear intent to get drunk, very drunk, and fast on top of it. Most students whom I asked cannot explain the allure of this habit. But there it is. What to do?

I fear that draconian threats of penalty will not be very effective. The prohibition era taught us that much. I expect better results from education. So far our educational efforts have concentrated on pointing out the effects of alcohol overuse. We have never earnestly tried to educate our young ones in responsible and moderate use of alcohol. We have largely criminalized alcohol consumption, and most state laws still allow our youths to have children, get married, or serve in the military, before we allow them to drink a glass of beer in a restaurant. Sex, driving a car, going to war—yes. The only area that remains taboo for young men and women is alcohol. Then, from one day to the next, usually on their 21st birthday, we expect young people to deal with alcohol responsibly. Whoever thought this approach would work?!

As a child, I saw wine and beer used moderately by my elders, and occasionally, beginning in my early teenage years, I was regularly invited to share a glass of wine, in younger years diluted, at the dinner table. When I entered college, drinking in public was no big deal for me and my peers. We had been drinking publicly and modestly with our own parents and relatives, not secretly with equally inexperienced high school or college buddies in back alleys and back seats of cars. Alcohol was not a rite of passage.

I think our own families ought to initiate our offspring into the proper use of alcohol. We should bring drinking out of the back alleys and dark bars into the well-lit parlors and dining rooms of our homes. We should as parents and relatives demonstrate that responsible drinking is possible and appropriate on many social occasions. We should bring consuming alcohol into the open where we can enjoy its use, and where we can observe and warn before things get out of hand. Colleges all by themselves cannot curb what has become a very serious problem. Families, friends, and society at large must become involved. It is worth a try. So far not much else has worked.

January 27, 1999

∼

Musings on bans, censorship, and biased rationale

We all hold dear notions of how the world should be, only to be taught by experience that, alas, our cherished perceptions don't always mesh with reality. I have long cradled the thought that university campuses are fertile grounds for new ideas, novel

47

approaches, bold experimentation: a laboratory of social concepts that advance our free society and improve the general state of humanity. However, bias, and preconceived notions thrive on university campuses just as well as in the rest of our society.

During my many years as a university president I received numerous letters from on and off campus, and often from very liberal quarters, with requests to ban, abolish, stifle, censor, or forbid. They recommended that I take actions which fly in the face of social open-mindedness and tolerance for divergent tastes and opinions. When it comes to personal, religious, or political biases, people who usually frown upon all forms of administrative interference will actually encourage presidential meddling and all sorts of censorship of opposing views.

While occasionally in accord with such biases, I erred usually on the side of tolerance and resisted the temptation to curtail activities in the social laboratory. I reflected bemusedly the other day on some of the requests I received and will list twenty of the most frequent suggestions and the accompanying rationale:

1. *Abolish parking for freshmen.* While hard on some (freshmen), it will alleviate parking problems for the rest of the campus population (juniors and seniors).

2. *Don't allow fatty foods to be served on campus.* They foster arteriosclerosis and are a health hazard.

3. *Abolish the Office of Lesbian, Bisexual and Gay services.* It is an abomination unto the Lord.

4. *Forbid the use of student hostesses for Football.* This will certainly lead to prostitution and demeans women, even if they volunteer for the program.

5. *Don't allow the drinking of beer or any other form of alcohol.* There is no responsible drinking. It may lead to alcoholism and thus nobody should drink.

6. *Don't allow a Christmas Tree on campus.* A public institution should not display religious symbols. If you must, at least

call the Christmas tree the "solstice bush."

7. *Don't allow a Black Miss WMU contest.* What would the African-American students say if we had an event that allowed only white women to participate?

8. *Ban the Wiccans from campus.* Witchcraft and devil worship have no room on campus.

9. *Speak out against nudity in theater performances.* The performances of the Theatre Department offend me. They often display frontal nudity which adds nothing to the plot or the message of the play.

10. *Forbid the burning of incense in dorm rooms.* The students do that only to mask the scent of marijuana.

11. *Abolish the invocation at commencement.* It may be fine in the U.S. Congress, but religious blessings have no place in public institutions.

12. *Reign in the out-of-control feminism on campus.* If men were to say the same unflattering things about women that feminists say about men, there would be a riot on campus.

13. *Stop planting flowers on campus.* They do not enhance learning and are a waste of money.

14. *Stop selling condoms on campus.* Students should not be given encouragement/ should not have sex at their age/ should remain chaste until they get married/ should have sex only off campus.

15. *Cut out the overdone research.* Universities are for teaching students, nothing else.

16. *Forbid Ebonics.* There is only one way to speak English.

17. *Ban the Greek system.* Fraternities and sororities are racially segregated, non co-ed, and drink too much.

18. *Raze Kanley Chapel.* It is a religious relic in the middle of a public school.

And finally, for good measure, my all time favorites:

19. *Do away with the outdoor sculptures on campus.* They are so abstract, no rational being can figure out what they represent. This is not art.

20. *Do away with the Bronco sculpture in front of Athletics.* It is so representational, everyone can see immediately what it is. This is not art.

If one ponders the list, one will no doubt find one or more items that meet one's own biases. But who would still want to be on our beautiful campus and in our intellectually rich university if all the above requests had been granted? Certainly not I.

March 17, 1999

≈

A tenured radical visits Kalamazoo

About forty years ago, I was teaching German language and literature to American students at the University of Munich. In 1961, I had in my classes a young woman whom I remember particularly well. She came from a wealthy Midwestern family, had attended an exclusive boarding school in the East, and then entered Bryn Mawr. She spoke German quite well, and I remember her as looking cute in the local Bavarian dirndl dresses. Ten years later, a bomb exploded in the basement of an elegant New York townhouse. When 57 sticks of dynamite were found on the site, it became obvious that Diana Oughton (this was my student's name) had accidentally blown herself up while making bombs. Only a fingertip was left of Diana, who had become a member of the radical Weathermen during the Vietnam War.

I was powerfully reminded of her the other day, when her former lover and fellow-radical, Bill Ayers, came to town to promote his book and to address students on Western's campus. The book, titled *Fugitive Days,* consists of Ayers' romanticized and utterly unapologetic reminiscences of the radical underground. The author describes the mayhem and destruction he created in the streets of Chicago, the bombings, his admiration for other terrorist leaders such as the infamous Bernadine Dohrn, and his successful flight from the FBI and justice.

Ayers still sounds elated when he recalls his anti-war marches in Chicago. "The crowd thundered down Clark, every window pane a target, every bit of glass in every business crashing joyously in our wake. With our pace now a dead run, some of us turned to car windows, hotel windows, the windows of the luxury high-rise apartments we streamed past. I swung my billy club into the windshield of a Cadillac and then a Mercedes." The book also describes how Ayers lifted wallets to finance his terrorist activities, how he obtained false IDs, and how he stole 125 pounds of high explosives. "It was illegal, yes, and dangerous, and the plans for the stuff apocalyptic. But we were freedom fighters..." he writes. Meanwhile, Bernadine Dohrn made the rounds among campus radicals preaching that the war must be brought home, by which she meant that the destruction and the violence of war had to be directed against the U.S. government and its representatives, the 'pigs.' Ayers also describes in detail how he and fellow terrorists placed and exploded a bomb in the Pentagon, and he justifies this terror act, in retrospect, as something that should be explained, and forgiven, by remembering the context of the times. Diana Oughton, Bill Ayers, and Bernadine Dohrn were certainly very dangerous persons as are all those who radicalize, without any restrictions, the political process.

Fugitive Days came out shortly before Muslim terrorists slammed planes into the World Trade Towers and the Pentagon. Ayers argues that while the Pentagon "dropped tens of thousands of pounds of explosives on Vietnam," his own bomb in the

Pentagon (three pounds of dynamite) was only "itsy-bitsy." Because nothing justified the Pentagon's actions in the Weathermen's calculus, "nothing could contradict the merit of ours."

I beg to differ. While I strongly support political protest and free speech, I fail to see any "merit" in throwing bombs, no matter how itsy-bitsy they are. And the argument that America's alleged violence abroad deserves to be countered with bombing federal buildings sounds too much like the hollow justifications of our radical Muslim attackers.

But nobody can call Bill Ayers a terrorist any longer. After all, he is now a Distinguished Professor of Education and Senior University Scholar at the University of Illinois in Chicago where he trains future generations of teachers for our public schools. His wife is Bernadine Dohrn, who wanted to violently overthrow the U.S. government and who tried to bring the terror of war to the streets of America. As a professor of law at Northwestern University, she now trains our next generation of lawyers and judges. When Bill and Bernadine now go out in Chicago, they no longer plant bombs or smash the windshields of cars. They now plant their ideas into young minds, perhaps the most effective form of subversive activity.

June 12, 2002

≈

II. English as a Second Language:
Observations of an Immigrant Nitpicker

Are there crimes against the English language any more?

Who would've thunk it? Initially, I had many reservations about offering comments in this column about misuses of grammar and syntax, but every time I write about the English language, reader mail starts flowing. I had expected that there would be one or two other fuddy-duddies who still appreciate the correct and precise usage of our tongue, but no: It appears that many more people than one commonly thinks are concerned with the proper use of English. On this issue I receive mail from senior citizens and pupils, from bankers, artists, homemakers, engineers, teachers, and accountants. All of them ask that I write additional columns about language use, and all of them offer their own linguistic pet peeves.

I have to be careful, of course. First of all, I do make mistakes myself and can't ride on too high a horse. And second, I can't forget what my friend Ilse Lehiste, a very distinguished linguistics professor at Ohio State, tried to hammer into me; namely that a living language changes, develops, mutates, and redesigns itself constantly, and that if enough people accept a new grammatical or syntactical usage, it becomes part of the language. She said, in short, that there is no such thing as correct or incorrect use of English; there are only different, and perfectly legitimate, ways of using the language. Well, excuse me, Ilse. I know you are right, but you can't tell me nothing no longer anymore. How is that for 'living' language?

So here comes some more nitpicking, just for the heck of it. On August 3, I opened the *Gazette* and found on page 5A a giant ad placed by an agency of the U.S. government, the Food and Drug Administration. It shows the faces of eleven children, most of them minorities, and the text reads: "Every day, 3000 kids become regular smokers. One of every three will die from it."

Then, under three of the faces, the captions read: "Will it be him?" "Will it be her?"

Will it be "him" who will die from it? Every sensitive ear aches to hear: 'Will it be *he* who dies from it?' Why would anyone use 'him' in this case? Who would say: 'It is him who is hungry'? or 'It is them who invited us'? (The subject of the sentence must be in the nominative case, the grammarian notes.) Deduct three points from the Food and Drug Administration. They should know better.

But wait! Each one of us, when asked who was knocking on the door, has at least occasionally responded: 'It is me.' The purist would indeed have to answer: 'It is I (who is knocking on the door).' Even I give this grammatically correct response seldom and only when I knock on the door of certain English professors.

Should I skate further out on thin ice and comment on another related problem? Here it is: Who and whom—a vexing problem for many speakers of English. 'Who did you invite'? would appear to many as proper English although one should correctly say: 'Whom did you invite'? 'Who did invite you'? asks which person gave you the invitation, whereas 'Whom did you invite'? asks for the person to whom you gave the invitation. That is exactly why we hear increasingly: 'He invited my brother and I,' or 'Just between you and I,' or even 'I bought a present for he and she.' (Ouch! That one really hurts.) It used to be easy. When in doubt if it is 'he' or 'him' or 'I' or 'me,' so I was taught, one merely needs to ask 'who?' or 'whom?' However, if he or she no longer knows the difference between 'who' and 'whom,' then the proper answer doesn't come any longer to he or she.

Not to worry, says Ilse.

August 11, 1999

∼

PC crusade mauls grammar

Were I to win the lottery, I would establish a well-endowed prize for teachers who still instruct their students in the old-fashioned basics of grammar.

In my German language courses, I spend too much of my

time teaching college freshmen plain English grammar. I can no longer assume that high school graduates are familiar with even basic grammatical terminology. Only with great hesitation do I throw out terms like 'adverb,' 'possessive pronoun,' or 'transitive verb,' realizing full well that most of my students are no more familiar with these terms than they are with the trainstops of the Trans-Siberian Railroad.

Last semester I prepared a lesson on the use of the personal pronoun. I explained that in German, as in English, a pronoun must agree in person, number, and gender with its antecedent, as in 'Henry loves his father' or 'These people need their heads examined.' But I met some blank stares. Why? Many of my students use personal pronouns incorrectly, following an unfortunately wide-spread trend.

And how can I blame them? When it comes to pronouns, our linguistic environment is flooded with grammatical monstrosities. I'll give just a few randomly collected examples. Our payroll department announces that: "All benefit eligible employees will receive an adjustment to your annual leave balance." It hurts to read that. The Computer Center writes: "If your student does not know their unified account name, they should go to the lab." My student not knowing 'their' account name? Should it perhaps be 'names'? And 'my student' followed by 'they'? That one hurts even more. The writers are college people, for Pete's sake! A union representative on PBS opens a session: "We will allow each participant to introduce themselves and tell us where they are from." Expect long speeches where each participant makes several introductions. A parent comments on the superintendent search: "I would have thought that they had taken the candidate they interviewed and hired them." How many superintendents should they have hired? The *Western Herald* opines that "A student must broaden their mind." One mind per student is usually all I ask for. James Carville, neither an English major nor a gentleman, advises: "It is hard for somebody to hit you when you've got a fist in their face." The *Gazette* tells us that "Anyone can vote in the primary if they are registered." The writer must be from Cook County where one allegedly votes early and often. And a State senator advises: "What's important is how much someone drinks, not what kind of person they are." Obviously, he expects multiple personalities.

I keep collecting examples of such linguistic misdemeanors, and they are legion. While they make me shudder, they roll smoothly off the tongues of even educated speakers and are to be found in print everywhere.

The reason for this irritating sloppiness lies, of course, in our almost fanatical desire to produce politically correct speech. Getting enraged by the appearance of a 'he' in a sentence where a 'she' would also be possible, some people see a need to sacrifice grammatical correctness on the altar of sensitivity. That's why we frequently see 'he/she' or 's/he;' the latter I don't even know how to pronounce. But even 's/he' still has the offensive odor of gender, whereas 'they' is gender neutral. So 'they' is used liberally, even where it is wrong. It is less dangerous to offend English grammar than the crusading PC?

What to do? First, the clumsiness of 'he/she' or 's/he' can usually be avoided by recasting the sentence using a plural antecedent and pronoun, as in: "Students who don't know their accounts..." Second, let's remember that 'anyone, everybody, each, someone etc.' are singular, regardless of the fact that many people see double when they hear these words and use 'they' and 'them' in connection with them. But lastly, writing that every employee will get 'your' annual leave balance is not sensitive; it is plain wrong English. At least that's what I am still trying to teach my students.

February 14, 2001

~

In a world of crazy political correctness, may we still be allowed proper English?

The story is by now pretty well known: In January of 1999, David Howard, head of the Office the Public Advocate in Washington, D.C., informed two of his subordinates, one white, one black, that the next budget would be tight. "I will have to be niggardly with this fund," he said, "because it's not going to be a lot of money." Marshal Brown, the black staff member, stormed out of the office before he could be advised of the word's meaning. When complaints about using a racial slur poured in, Mr. Howard offered his resignation, and the city's new mayor accepted it.

One can safely assume that neither Mr. Brown nor the mayor knew the meaning and etymology of the word. Although not widely used, the word 'niggardly' nevertheless regularly appears in reports and editorials meaning 'miserly' or 'stingy' and has, of course, not the slightest etymological relation to the dreaded N-word that Mr. Brown mistakenly identified.

After outrage and ridicule had been heaped on Washington's mayor, his spokesperson announced that Mr. Howard would be brought back into city government, but not to the same high profile position. No word about what happened to Mr. Brown who so ignorantly took offense. I think he should be condemned to take a few more English classes of which probably even the mayor would benefit.

Just after I had convinced myself that this was merely one of the many crazy stories coming out of Washington, I was struck again by the same word. Only this time it came from the University of Wisconsin, a highly selective university and arguably one of the best in the country. A young woman, president of the Wisconsin Black Student Union, so the *Chronicle of Higher Education* reported, appeared before the Faculty Senate to announce her offense at the use of the word 'niggardly' by her professor in his Introduction to British Literature course.

While discussing the *Canterbury Tales,* her professor had characterized one of the figures in the prologue as niggardly. "I didn't know what it meant," the student testified. "I found out later, but it didn't take away from the offensiveness." She talked to her professor who explained that he did in no way mean to offend her, and that the word had no connection whatsoever with a racial slur. However, the student still expected that the word would not be used again in class because she felt offended by its sound.

Assuming that other members of his class might also be unfamiliar with the word, the professor explained the word's meaning and etymology at the beginning of the next class and also referred to the story of Mr. Howard's Washington dilemma. The student took particular offense at the fact that the professor used the word again in class after she had told him of her objection, and she entered a public protest.

Reading these reports, I had to take a deep breath. What in the world is happening here? Has PC gone mad? A mayor accepts the resignation of a person and then demotes him because the subordinate has a richer knowledge of their common native tongue? A student in a university English class wants to prevent her professor from using a perfectly good word because she is offended by its sound, not its meaning? A professor must fear to offend the 'sensitivity' of a student because he uses his class time to explain a finer point of the English lexicon? And all this does not happen in some little backward town but in our nation's capital and in one of our country's elite universities? One shudders at the thought. What better argument could one make for more English education in our schools and for more rigorous admission standards to our best universities!

In the middle of all this commotion, the Wisconsin Faculty Senate debated and subsequently changed its heretofore strict speech code which threatened faculty with discipline for using speech that "makes the instructional setting hostile or intimidating." Recognizing that "the maintenance of intellectual freedom through the open expression of ideas will sometimes be unavoidably hurtful," the Wisconsin faculty nevertheless asserted in its new code that the principle of academic freedom requires that all thoughts germane to the subject matter of the course must be protected by the freedom of speech and thus must be free from disciplinary action.

On Wisconsin, on Wisconsin!

April 7, 1999

~

58

Is trying for gender correctness linguistic nitpicking?

Many years ago, I received an award that embarrasses me to this day. I was then dean of the large College of Humanities at Ohio State and had recently introduced a new policy regarding due process in cases of student complaints. When it was issued, a group who held the PC franchise on campus, commended me "for linguistic sensitivity in addressing gender issues in official college documents."

The document in question read somewhat like this:

"A student who wishes to register a complaint about his/her class, will bring his/her complaint to her/his instructor and discuss with him/her her/his concerns. Only after he/she is unable to solve the issue with her/his instructor will he/she approach her/his chairperson to discuss his/her problem with her/him..." And so on.

Those who praised me for my linguistic sensitivity were pleased that I not only used both the female and male personal pronoun but that I alternated them regularly. How sensitive, indeed.

I assure everyone that I am not he/she who wrote those abominable sentences. Between committee meeting and typesetting some well-meaning person must have 'improved' the text up to proper PC standards.

The concern at the time was most appropriate and understandable. Many women felt excluded when practically all university publications used the male personal pronoun exclusively, and I often wondered why this matter had not been raised earlier. After all, half of our students at that time were women, and in the College of Humanities their percentage was even higher.

But the linguistic dilemma can be addressed so much more easily. If the noun is changed into its plural, the male and female personal pronouns become indistinguishable. Two goals can be served with one little change: the gender concern can be properly addressed, and our English language won't be tortured. The text should have read: "Students who wish to register complaints about their classes will bring these concerns to their class instructors and discuss these with them." And so on. Very easy. The text is now gender neutral. Everyone is happy.

But no! A new linguistic goblin has crept in, and it has already become so pervasive that I begin to catch myself using it occasionally. It may not be a big deal, but it is grammatically incorrect, even if the governor uses it, too.

A Midwestern governor is quoted in *U.S. NEWS* as follows: "A child growing up unable to read or to do mathematics...will be disenfranchised...throughout their life." How does 'a child' refer to the pronoun 'their'? And if 'their' is right, shouldn't it then also be 'lives'?

This politician is not alone, of course. In a full-page ad in *The Chronicle of Higher Education*, a college professor proclaims: "If a student passes this Regent's College exam... they know as much about the subject as one who participates in my class..."

One can find this and similar usage everywhere and certainly in conversational English. I assume it reflects the speaker's attempt to focus caringly on the specific person ('each individual child,' as in the governor's example) while at the same time generalizing the impact of educational neglect. Or does the speaker try to avoid the admittedly awkward 'she/he' possibility? Again: using the noun in the plural solves the problem grammatically. "All children growing up unable to read...will be disenfranchised...throughout their lives." Nothing simpler than that.

Is this nitpicking? Or, put differently: Should anyone thinking about such grammatical problems have "their" head examined?

My friend, the noted art historian Bernard Goldman, has resolved the gender issue by signing his correspondence: "Bernard Goldperson." I appreciate his humorous sentiment, but who would accept his personal check with that signature?

May 19, 1999

∾

Latin and Greek—any chance of using both properly?

During the week of the Medieval Congress on Western's campus, I am often drawn back into memories of my school days when Latin was heavy on my school agenda. Being university bound meant, in those days, taking a heavy dose of Latin and a little Greek on the side.

I can't say I disliked learning it. Although considered a dead language, Latin could be a lot of fun. Once a basic mastery was achieved, we began to comprehend semi-risqué Latin jokes, usually of a sexual nature and of the type that amuses the pubescent mind. And they do stick in one's memory beyond puberty. While visiting a school chum last month, we remembered quite a few of them and roared with laughter. Our wives smiled forgivingly.

Latin made us little boys and girls special. For me Latin was the first 'other' language, and it was a wondrous experience to learn that the same objects could have different names and that complex thoughts could be transported in different linguistic vessels. Latin also opened the world of ancient gods and demigods, fabulous heroes, and famous battles and wars.

When I graduated from high school, my infatuation with gods and mythical heroes had waned, and my Latin teachers appeared to have become successively meaner. For my graduating exam my teacher selected a piece of medieval Church-Latin, much more complex than classical Latin, a papal encyclical in which the pope sternly warned against the use of the crossbow, which he saw as a new weapon of mass destruction. Hiroshima had happened a few years prior to my graduation. The medieval pope's concern had been put in its proper perspective.

Latin made me a pretty good speller (given the enormous wealth of Latin roots in English); it allows me to read inscriptions on tombstones in medieval cathedrals and on old buildings; and it has taught me the nomenclature and basics of grammar. (Big deal, my children will say, and they are not altogether wrong.) It has also made me allergic to the grammatically incorrect use of Latin words and expressions of which English has so many.

May I list just a few? Let me begin with my favorite example, a word that is irremovable from our modern vocabulary. The word is 'data.' It appears almost exclusively in its plural form meaning broadly 'facts' (or 'the givens'). Since it is plural in its form, it demands the plural verb form, as in: 'Your data ARE wrong,' (not 'is') or 'The data HAVE no significance' (not 'has'). However, the incorrect usage is already so entrenched that I have little hope of a turnaround.

In the same category is the word 'media.' We hear, 'The media has told us for years…,' and I wince. The print press is one 'medium,' the radio and television are others. All of them together make up the 'media' in its plural form. It would be nice to hear once in a while that 'one medium, the print press, HAS reported the data accurately whereas the other media HAVE not.' 'Medium' and 'media' are more often used correctly in their singular and plural form than 'data,' I think.

Dare I mention a third item? 'Criteria' and 'criterion'? The same problem here with the incorrect use of singular and plural. Who has not heard a remark like: 'Competence IS the main criteria'? There never is one main 'criteria,' only one main 'criterion.' Criteria (plural) are always more than one, or else they shrink to one individual (singular) criterion.

Does it all matter? Perhaps not much, but it is always pleasing if people use language precisely. And those who don't give a hoot, would you please at least humor this old nitpicker by not saying 'ek cetera.' This one we can get right: It is 'et cetera' –clearly with a ' t.' Please!

June 23, 1999

∽

Waiting for the miracle of baby's first words

One of the greatest miracles in our lives is the development of speech. Parents can't wait to hear baby's first gurgles and murmurs and celebrate the first time a toddler says an intelligible word. My little granddaughter Stefanie babbles all day long and produces cute sounds but, alas, these sounds are not yet words to be found in the dictionary. At this time she only converses with our neighbor's dog to which she barks and that responds in kind. Any day now, her parents and we say to each other, any day now she will say something to us, and all of us secretly hope that this first word will be our own name. Such are the vanities of grandparents and parents.

All my life I have been intrigued by the linguistic development of children. We observe in awesome wonder their acquisition of speech—single words first and then little amazing sentences which create pride and utter delight in the older generation. Proud mothers will make long distance calls to their own mothers to announce the arrival of these first words; and grandmothers listen to these sweet sounds with unconcealed emotion.

I wish we could keep this great sense of miracle and accomplishment alive beyond the baby years. It seems that many parents, once the little tykes have begun to speak intelligibly, lose their keen interest in their children's language development and with it their sense of the wonder of human speech. And perhaps understandably so. Once little Bobby and Mary have learned to speak, there are so many other admirable skills they acquire— eating properly, painting, reading, throwing balls—and these attract parental attention and pride to such a degree that our early focus on language takes a back seat. Would that it never did.

Occasionally, while watching TV interviews from England, I am impressed with how articulate many middle class people appear and what pride they seem to place in the proper use of their language. Many of us have experienced the extreme respect most French display and expect for their native tongue. However, I think we as a nation do not cherish language to the same degree as some other countries. Perhaps we are more relaxed as a people in general; perhaps in our very pragmatic American ways we think that the main point is to get the message across, no matter how poorly or how well packaged. Perhaps. I wish I knew.

I just know that when it comes to linguistic sophistication and precision we could and we should do a lot better. I find that the communication skills of many of our high school and college students ought to be more refined and polished. As a college teacher I observe daily how my students struggle to find adjectives beyond 'cool' or 'awesome' when asked to describe an event, a movie, a book, a meal, or another person.

Granted, quite a few students handle language well (Thanks, parents and teachers everywhere!), but I frown when I observe how pervasively crude and foul some conversations have become. In the speech of some youngsters (and some of their elders) the F-word is the preferred adjective, equally suited to describe the f...g paycheck, the f...g weather, or f...g politics. This mindless obscenity rolls smoothly off the tongues of people and, in many circles, no longer offers offense. Where have all the mothers gone who prescribed washing out mouths with soap on such occasions?

But many of us love language and would like to see it handled more gracefully. We should keep the wonder of language development alive beyond the toddler years. Let us show and teach our children that language can do more than carry simple messages and content. Let us show them that it can charm, amuse, and enchant; that it can stimulate both speaker and listener; and that it is rich and enriching and seemingly inexhaustible in all its marvelous possibilities.

October 27, 1999

~

Is my mother-in-law a guy?

I remember exactly the first time I heard it. About fifteen years ago, the door bell rang, my wife opened, and a nice little boy, about eight years old, asked: "Would you guys buy some cookies for our basketball team?" We did.

Since then the address for two or more persons, regardless of gender, seems to have become 'You guys.' Waiters approach my wife, my eighty-six year old mother-in-law, and me and ask: "What can I bring you guys?" I find it hard to think of my wife as a guy and even harder when it comes to my mother-in-law who dates back to a time when adults were addressed as 'Mr.' and 'Mrs.,' perhaps even as 'Sir' and 'Ma'am.' *Tempi passati.* Now it is 'you guys' (in some restaurants 'you folks'), and one almost has to travel to the deep South to hear an occasional 'Sir' or

'Ma'am' or go to a rather elegant restaurant where the wait staff is still trained before it is let loose on the customers.

I know that the young people who serve my food in most restaurants don't mean to be discourteous when using this form of address. Awful as it may sound to my ears, it is so widely used, and accepted, that only a fool would take offense. And so I don't. But from any restaurant that promises 'fine dining,' I expect better. The moment I pay a substantial price for a meal, I expect more class and a better linguistic ambience than 'you guys' or 'you folks.'

Luckily, in this country, he who dines is left with some defenses. In Germany, for instance, a 15% gratuity is included in the bill, which leaves the diner defenseless against poor service. We Americans still enjoy the unalienable right to determine the size of the tip, and the waiters realize that. I am known as a generous tipper and tip gladly, but I do run into disagreements occasionally with my wife and children because I don't accept poor service without comment. Particularly when my children were in their teenage/embarrassment stage they unfailingly admonished me every time we entered a restaurant not to make incommodious comments to the waiter. They preferred that, if I must, I should wield the silent sword of defense by tipping poorly. But I don't want to be seen as a miser; I want the waiter to know why I am tipping niggardly.

Folksy forms of address are not restricted to restaurants, of course. I feel considerable resentment, for instance, when a physician approaches my hospital bed and introduces himself: "Hi, Diether. I'm Dr. Meyers." When I discussed such approaches once with the dean of our medical school, asking him to teach his young charges to be more sensitive, he told me that most patients, usually distressed in a hospital setting, feel more comfortable and relaxed when addressed by their first name. Again, I seem to be the exception, because it only increases my blood pressure. And I don't even have the defense of the lowered tip since gratuities, in this setting, are clearly included in the price.

In my own professional setting, the transition to greater folksiness has also entered the lecture hall. Ever increasing numbers of college professors, some of them the age of their charges' grandparents, encourage their students to call them by their first names. Whether or not that really brings their students closer to them and improves their learning I dare not say, although I strongly doubt it. In fact, I guess that a large number of students might even be uncomfortable with such forced familiarity. Would we want them to walk into their first job interview later and call their employers 'John and Mary' or 'you guys'?

Does it all matter? Not all that much, I think. It will remain a case of personal preference. But to all those waiters and waitresses out there: Omitting the 'you guys' will get you an additional 5% from me. Think about it!

July 1, 1999

∾

Incensed at 'incent'? Don't decool as I present

A living language is something marvelous because, like a living organism, it may grow, change, or mutate and thus remain fresh and surprising. It appears that young speakers especially enjoy experimenting with language, often adding new words to it or changing the meaning of words and concepts. The word 'cool' for instance was once quite plain in its meaning. It then took a meaning signifying relaxed attitude and behavior. But now it is widely used as an adjective suitable to describe practically anything: a person, a movie, a concert, an idea—you name it. In fact it is so widely used that I often think the speaker knows only this one adjective and no other. While it was an enriching innovation initially, the word's current undiscriminating use begins to empty it of any but the most general meaning. I predict it will eventually disappear from being in vogue like so many other words that I remember from the forties and fifties which now cause blank stares in teenagers.

Lately I have been wondering about the innovative use of verbs. I was always uncomfortable when a stewardess told me to 'deplane' the aircraft. I know that one can debone a chicken, but deplane an aircraft? Can I decar my automobile? Or dehouse my condominium? I don't like 'deplane' as a word, but I guess it is in our language to stay.

In the business world I have picked up a few other gems. A board on which I served was severing a business relationship, and we informed our partners that we were 'departicipating.' Is this more elegant or more polite than quitting, leaving, or ending our contract?

Similarly innovative is 'to incent,' meaning to provide incentives for employees. "Mary needs to be better incented," I recently read in some board materials. Should I feel incensed?

At another board meeting we were asked to take out our calendars because the administration wanted 'to calendar a project.' Clearly another good one!

At yet another occasion we were not given a gift but accepted a 'gifted house.' Whatever happened to the verb 'to donate'? No longer good enough? Up to that point I had only heard of 'gifted children,' which of course did not mean they were left on our doorsteps.

However, the university is just as innovative as the business world. It employs people who are 'siting a building,' i.e. finding the right place for it. Or when a faculty member provides liaison to another governing body, I now hear frequently that 'Bob will liaise' to the executive committee. Poor Bob!

But the most questionable item to me is when a transitive verb is changed into an intransitive one without any good reason whatsoever. It may be pure laziness. The case in point is 'to present' which is transitive and takes a direct object as in: 'He presented a paper.' But the widely accepted use on campuses these days is: 'I was at a conference and presented.' Or: 'Last year Bob presented several times.' Presented what? I ask. His face? His opinion? A paper, perhaps?

What is it with us nitpickers that we feel rubbed the wrong way by such innocent little linguistic glitches? I guess we simply enjoy noticing how language changes and like to comment on it. On the other hand: If someone properly incented me I would perhaps demare my high horse and decomment on linguistic topics.

January 26, 2000

∼

English pronunciation is confusing for the immigrant

In my eulogy for Maestro Yoshimi Takeda I mused about the distinctive accents that both of us, as immigrants from Japan and Germany, carried with us throughout our careers. Neither of us had to introduce himself by name on the phone to be immediately recognized. It amused both of us, and we were convinced that even heavy breathing would be enough to reveal our accented identities. After the memorial service a couple fondly remembered that their seven-year-old son once received a phone call from Maestro Takeda while they were out and reported that a Mr. Potato had called and left a message that the boy did not understand.

Linguistic miscommunications like this go both ways. I remember that during my early years in the United States I continually met people who came from places that I could not locate. I met people who claimed to be from Allana (Georgia), Loovul (Kentucky), Mwakee (Wisconsin), Balamer (Maryland) or Nerk (New Jersey). Others lived in the state of Iwa or Hia, which many New Yorkers take to be one and the same. There is an American tendency to slur sounds, and words that the immigrant knows perfectly well when he sees them written may become unrecognizable when elided. The word 'handbag' is usually pronounced 'hambag'—which could mean something entirely different. Few people iron a shirt; instead they 'iorn' it. Most Midwesterners walk 'acrosst' rather than across the street. And they do this not later, but 'lader.' All this the newcomer finds most 'inneresting.'

Trying to find Loovul on a map is one thing, but finding one's way through the bewildering jungle of English/American pronunciation is probably the immigrant's greatest challenge. First, there are some English sounds that are difficult to master, such as the 'l' that gives many Chinese problems and the 'th' that many Germans or Italians simply replace with a 'd.' Once these tongue twisters are overcome, other surprising and inexplicable mysteries arise before the learner of English.

As if by magic, certain letters seem to disappear or are rendered inaudible—even with unslurred speech. One never hears the 'b' in debt or doubt, or the 't' in whistle or the second 't' in thistle. Or one looks at two almost visually identical words and finds that the letter 'g' in 'singer' sounds different than the same letter in the word 'finger.' The difficult sound of 'th' is made more complicated by the fact that it can be pronounced in different ways as in 'thigh' and 'thy.' The same sequence of letters, let's say 'ough,' can be pronounced in many different ways as the words 'tough,' 'plough,' or 'dough' will demonstrate. And why is it 'ear' but 'early'? All this is quite confusing to someone who does not speak English as a native language.

But the mysteries do not end there. How hard to understand that words, which look very much alike, sound so different when they make the transition from letter to sound! How similar do these words look, and how different is their pronunciation: four and tour; low and how; five and give; ache and mustache; break and speak. And even more confusing: completely identical words can have not only different meanings but also different pronunciations: Lead (the metal) and lead (to guide); or the bow (and arrow) and the bow the actor takes; or the bass (fish) and the bass (instrument); or to polish a shoe and the Polish grandfather. To make the confusion for the immigrant perfect, words can even change their meaning depending on whether the accent rests on the first or the second syllable: I permit, and I obtain a permit.

I miss my friend Yoshimi and wish he were still around. Together we could continue to wonder endlessly about the peculiarities of English pronunciation.

August 22, 2000

~

Business leaders must demand literacy

A few years ago, I attended a conference at which business leaders told college administrators what skills and qualities they expected to find in our graduates and their future employees. High among the executives' concerns, as I remember, was that many of their junior managers no longer wrote or spoke effectively. I was not surprised.

Just one example: Prior to 1968, students at the University of California were automatically exempted from remedial English, known as 'Bonehead English,' if they scored higher than 600 on the English Achievement Test. Fewer than 35% of all students attended the Bonehead sections. In 1968, the score was reduced to 550. However, in spite of this significant easing of the score, the number of Bonehead freshmen increased to well over 50% in the seventies. In 1976, the University of California abolished remedial English and merged it with Freshman English. Once the majority of freshmen require remedial instruction, it is no longer labeled remedial. It becomes the accepted norm.

What has happened? Clearly, our students are every bit as talented as those of earlier generations. But they bring with them different skills. If I have a computer problem, I only need to open my office door and wait for the next undergraduate to walk by. Chances are 2:1 that the youngster can fix my dilemma within minutes. Chances are also 3:1 that the student won't be able to express himself in precise and coherent sentences. Bright though he is, he will speak what I call the 'I'm-kinda-like-you-know-what-I-mean' version of the current vernacular.

Over the last few decades we have de-emphasized the study of the humanities and the arts which, to a large extent, deal with and depend on verbal and written expression. There has been a bold shift towards technically oriented academic disciplines which are perceived as providing better chances for employment and, in a general sense, hold more of a future. As science and technology are getting ever more complex, four years are barely enough to provide a good undergraduate education in applied professional fields. Adding a humanities curriculum is hard to do, even though accrediting agencies in business and engineering increasingly demand it, and although industry CEOs give moving speeches on the necessity of a broad liberal education for the young people who enter their companies.

We in education would believe these words, but the personnel recruiters don't seem to hear the speeches their CEOs make. As long as industry recruiters systematically select people with very focused engineering, accounting, or computer skills, our students will not make any special efforts to enrich their education with courses that strengthen their writing and speaking. If industry needs and wants language skills, it must hire accordingly and cannot just pay cheap lip service to humanities education. If we want to preserve effective levels in communication, business and industry must help education. As the future employers of our graduates, they must demand these skills. Our students often listen to their future employers more carefully than to their professors.

Only a century ago, many people, educated and uneducated, wrote letters, extensive diaries, or painted. Thus they recorded and conveyed their thoughts, their elations and miseries, partly to provide themselves psychological relief through self-expression, but also to transmit to succeeding generations the essence of their spiritual existence. Our generation has succumbed to a technology that largely eliminates the contemplation that was necessary for the letter or the entry into the diary. We replaced the letter with the long-distance call and the diary with the photo album. Some publishers ask us to rewrite our college textbooks for the tenth grade reading level. They ask us to go for the easy, but wrong, solution. We should not further dumb down each text, nor should we agree to have our constitution, or the works of Walt Whitman, rewritten and simplified so that they remain intelligible for increasingly functionally illiterate people. We should be equally sophisticated in handling both our language and our technology.

The business and education communities must speak with one voice when it comes to raising our language skills. I consider this to be in our joint best interest.

February 28, 2001

∼

What too doe when the spellchecker fails?

When I grew up, I first learned to write and then to type. Then the computer appeared, the typewriter became the word processor, and sentences were no longer written but 'processed.' I intensely dislike that term and continue to write rather than process words. The computer has also introduced the option to 'spellcheck' our processed words, and my latest software even provides a 'grammarcheck' which mostly advises me that my sentences are too complex. Too complex for whom? For the eighth grade reader? I sometimes wonder which software engineer is setting the new standards for linguistic complexity. I have decided that I can live quite well without the grammarcheck.

The spellchecker, on the other hand, is a useful feature. Although I am a pretty good speller, I occasionally use a word that I am not quite certain how to spell. Is 'letter-perfect' one word, or is it hyphenated? Is it 'Baghdad' or 'Bagdad'? Better also check 'bandoleer.' In dozens of cases the spellchecker saves me a trip to the dictionary. This electronic feature also saves me from the genuine typo, and although I have ample experience in proofreading, an occasional typo does slip by; particularly if I am proofing a text that I typed or, excuse me, processed myself. The spellchecker will catch all the 'walkpapers' that were meant to be 'wallpapers' and the 'deades' that should have been 'decades.' A great help for the fast typist and the tired eye.

However, there are some typos that even the best spellchecker will not detect. When things are going fast, I often type 'he' when I mean 'the,' and I have typed 'litter' when in fact I meant 'letter.' As long as the typed word exists in English, the spellcheck feature abandons us, and the reader must decide if the writer made a typo or is an ignoramus. Some people, of course, suspect also a third possibility. Once I appointed a renowned specialist in public policy to a distinguished position in the university, but the official announcement, which I, of course, had not typed, said that he had been awarded the chair "in pubic affairs." Like many academics, very touchy and not without vanity, he chided me for what he believed was an intentional affront to his dignity.

The university, I have always claimed and demanded, should strive for clear and accurate use of English in all its publications and pronouncements. I find it embarrassing if a teaching institution is caught with incorrect use of the English language. Easier said than done. Even the most elevated officers in the academy sometimes stumble. I have heard a college president at commencement introduce the teaching staff with the line: "And here

72

behind me sit the men and women who compromise our faculty." I am sure he meant 'comprise.' A Freudian slip perhaps? A dean sent me an invitation to a lecture with the unusual promise: "Immediately after the presentation, a reception will be held at which refreshments will be severed." An art department (not WMU's) announced an exhibit at which we were to admire one of its painting professor's "rich and colorful palate." I felt like passing the invitation on to my dentist.

I am more forgiving when it comes to similar blunders by my students. In a recent course on ideal societies, a student claimed that "Adam and Eve were ejaculated from the Garden of Eden," not quite what I remembered had happened to them. Another one maintained that a temple of antiquity "was ravished by fire." Is that close enough? But I will not accept that Joan of Arc "was burned at the steak" nor do I accept the finding that "the professor emphasizes the histerical background too much." However, I was more inclined to forgive a student who stated that he "liked Dr. Haenicke's coarse very much." Not everyone felt that way. Another student complained that "Dr. Haenicke does not have enough patients." That is indeed true, particularly when it comes to such atrocious spelling.

March 21, 2002

～

Experiencing my writing process at this point in time

This morning, I cut myself shaving. I was listening to PBS. An economist had been asked if, in his expert opinion, he expected the stock market to improve soon. "Not soon," he replied, "but in the not too far distant future." I hate it when an intelligent person talks in such contorted language and with such imprecision. I have run into economists before who deliberately want to be imprecise when such questions are asked of them. I would settle, in such cases, for a simple 'I don't know,' or even the vague, 'It will turn around sooner or later,' but, 'in the not too far distant future' is the linguistic equivalent of walking on stilts—and stumbling.

But our experts and consultants love to put on linguistic stilts whenever they give us their high-priced opinions, obviously thinking that what they say sounds more learned, profound, or expert if they frame simple concepts in complex terms. I am convinced that an expert is unable to say simply, 'now' or, 'right now.' Instead he will say, 'at this point in time' or, 'at this moment in time,' two overblown expressions that ought to trigger a reduced consulting fee for the speaker.

I am similarly surprised when people open their presentations with the words: 'Frankly, let me be honest with you,' or, 'to be perfectly honest,' or, 'to tell you the truth.' Does he who speaks this way need to announce that his statements, for once, will be truthful? Am I to trust any other of the speaker's remarks, not prefaced by the reassuring 'honestly'? Is this speaker usually duplicitous, but not 'at this point in time'? Or is this opening statement meant to attract my special attention, because now I will hear the truth, which the speaker usually does not dispense? Or is this phrase just a thoughtless linguistic habit? Most likely the latter, but it makes me wonder each time.

Another favorite of experts is the word 'experience.' They claim that through architectural changes they can improve the customer's dining experience; they promise that new lighting will enhance the client's banking experience; they describe the enriched reading experience in the renovated library; and most certainly the students will have a better learning experience in the new labs. However, they also test, with such unnecessary verbiage, my listening experience. Why does every good activity—such as reading, dining, and learning—have to become an experience? If we don't stop this word, we'll soon hear about the walking experience, the sleeping experience, and the kissing experience.

Another word very much in vogue is 'process,' both as a noun and as a verb. No, you can't think about it any more—you have to process the information. I have been told that people are processing their grief, or they are processing a thought. The paper that is due is not yet done, but the student is involved in the writing process. Happy and positive thoughts, so I am told, accelerate the healing process. Processing seems to make the grieving or thinking or writing appear so much more tangible. There is activity in processing, and visible results can be expected, just as when I am putting carrots into my food processor.

Want it or not, we all tend to use these terms because we are deluged with them day in, day out. In most cases, we develop a lazy toierance for their use and almost become unaware of their intrusion into our speech patterns. However, when these patterns become too repetitive and begin to overwhelm us, we register negative reactions. I am at that point now and think that 'process' and 'experience' are overused and need a good, long rest. Other stilted phrases, such as 'at this moment in time,' are just too silly and pretentious and deserve to be put out of commission indefinitely. Perhaps they will experience a disappearing process as have so many other expressions that were in vogue at one point in time. To be honest, if they do, I promise my grieving process will be brief.

January 23, 2002

~

Good English is the most important work tool

I always write my columns about the correct use of the English language with some trepidation; mainly because I am not the ultimate authority on the subject and am apt to make mistakes myself. But then, I do enjoy it when people speak English well and correctly, and I certainly encourage good and effective writing and speaking among the students I teach. I think every teacher should do the same. Therefore I am sometimes in disagreement with English teachers, both on the K-12 and the college level, who dismiss my insistence on correct grammar and syntax. Some of them argue strongly that as long as the speaker gets his message across and is understood by the listener, all is fine and correcting grammar and style is nothing but magisterial condescension. Besides, it is often claimed, English is a living language in which rules of grammar and the meaning of words shift and change, and, therefore, there is no such thing as wrong use of the language.

Well, I am happy to say, I beg to differ. Even my pre-school granddaughter gets her message across, but that should not be enough for a more advanced student. People have to communicate well and on a level appropriate for their age. And while I realize that a language undergoes constant change and innovation, I do not readily accept imaginative spelling and the bending of accepted standards of grammar. In fact, I think that most students would be much better prepared for college if they had received a more generous dose of grammar and syntax in high school.

So I let the red ink flow when I meet with 'wrong grammar' in term papers and essays. One pattern is already deeply engrained in the speech of many people. It is the wrong use of the past form (gave) when the past participle (given) is needed. For instance, I do not accept 'he could have came,' or 'I would have gave him the money,' although the pattern is in wide use. You can find it in print in our local *Enterprise* magazine ("I've always came up with the same answer") or hear Phil Donahue say on his show: "We were shook." Plain wrong in my book and a terror to my ears.

Another expression, widely used, but usually in the wrong way, is 'hopefully.' It deserves to be eradicated in its current usage, but I confess that chances for that to happen are nil. 'Hopefully' is commonly found in sentences such as: 'Hopefully the weather will be nice on Sunday. Hopefully we can go to the picnic. Hopefully the stock market will recover.' Everyone has heard such and similar phrases, and to my shame I admit that I catch myself occasionally using them, too.

Of course, we all know that we have depersonalized the former 'I hope' and replaced it with the impersonal 'hopefully.' Hopefully actually means 'full of hope' or 'filled with hope.' We should therefore say: 'I hope the weather will be nice on Sunday, and I hope the stock market will recover.' 'Hopefully' should be used in sentences like: 'She read the letter hopefully, searching for the words she wanted to hear,' and 'Hopefully he invested a large sum in the enterprise.' In this case the linguists' argument has almost won me over: the use of 'hopefully' is changing before our eyes, and the wide, although 'wrong,' usage of the expression has made it acceptable. I still mark it, though.

Do I drive my students nuts with my nitpicking, or do I do them a favor? I hope it is the latter. In job interviews, most employers will be impressed by those who speak English well and correctly. It always made a difference with me when I hired people. When my students write their first on-the-job reports, someone will take note that they can express themselves succinctly. In fact, I think that all my nitpicking and correcting helps my students to sharpen and to use skillfully the most important tool with which they will ever work. Hopefully!

August 28, 2002

∼

Words become meaningless with misuse

A finalist for the position of fire chief in Ann Arbor is under grand jury investigation in Georgia because of alleged corruption in his department. But he called the accusations against him "just a bunch of rhetoric—it don't mean anything." Granted, the man isn't trying to be hired as an English teacher, so I won't chide him for his poor grammar. At least he did not say, "It don't mean nothing," which is another frequently used statement in circles where proper English is considered the province of incurable nerds. No, I am picking on the word 'rhetoric.'

The hopeful applicant uses the word to describe the allegations against him as balderdash and baseless gossip. But rhetoric actually denotes just the opposite. Rhetoric was once the art of using language well and persuasively and was taught as an academic discipline concerned with the principles of effective communication. Preachers, politicians, teachers, and other public speakers devoted themselves to the study of rhetoric, hopeful of reaching higher levels of eloquence. But as the art of public speaking fell into neglect, the word rhetoric underwent a similar descent and is now misused—not only by prospective fire chiefs—as meaning empty speech. A once proud concept—artful communication—has been degraded to denoting nonsense.

I stumble quite often across words whose meanings have been severely corrupted. The other day, a theater critic praised an actor for having delivered 'an incredible performance.' Incredible actually means something so implausible as to elicit disbelief. I am certain that the actor tried very hard to give a credible performance, but these days one must assume it is praise when hearing that a political candidate 'gave an incredible speech.' An object can advance with incredible speed, but a politician's speech better be credible, or else it might be perceived as 'just a bunch of rhetoric.'

The adjective 'terrific' has also been distorted into its exact opposite. Since it actually means causing terror and great fear, a Halloween mask would appropriately be described as terrific, and so I wonder if I should be upset when someone finds that I look terrific. Clearly, though, most people using the word do not think of its original root meaning and are paying the terrific-looking person a compliment.

The word 'delicious' is also now frequently used in contexts that go against my linguistic sensibilities. To me the word means pleasing to the senses, especially of taste or smell, and so I find a meal, a wine or its bouquet delicious. However, I still can't bring myself to find a poem, a new suit, a painting, or a woman delicious. I make an exception when it comes to pairing the adjective with the noun revenge: there is something like delicious revenge.

Many good words are simply used carelessly by the media and thus emptied of real meaning. Reporters repeatedly called the trucker who spotted the car of the suspected Washington snipers a 'hero.' Not a good choice of words. Recognizing a license plate and calling 911 are not heroic acts. Let's save that precious word for those who risk their lives in the service of others.

Similarly, when the two alleged snipers were identified, TV commentators questioned if "these two gentlemen" had appropriate legal representation. I thought gentlemen were men with great consideration for others and high standards of proper behavior. If media parlance prevails, we soon will not only have gentlemen farmers, but also gentlemen snipers.

At Senator Wellstone's funeral, one of the speakers challenged the audience "to redeem the sacrifice of Paul Wellstone's death" by voting for Walter Mondale. Setting aside the gross tastelessness of turning a funeral into a political rally, the senator's death was not a sacrifice. It was a horrible and saddening accident, and those who perished in the crash certainly did not mean to sacrifice their lives for votes.

It troubles me that TV and print journalists are sometimes so careless with language. Overuse, misuse, and reckless hype tend to empty out the solid meaning of good words. If simple actions become heroism and each plane crash a sacrifice, we soon won't have any proper words left when we encounter the real article.

November 6, 2002

∾

Chewing the fat with a couple of cats

When I was still young and ambitious and began to travel, I made it a point to prepare myself linguistically for each trip. Prior to a journey to Italy, I would enroll in an Italian course so I could learn enough to ask for the way to a museum, order a drink, or ask for the check in a restaurant. When formal language study was impossible, I used to buy special books that introduced frequently used phrases and their pronunciation in other languages. I rarely crossed a European border at that time without having memorized at least the numbers in, say, Greek or Danish, and I could exchange simple greetings and say 'thank you' and 'please.' Such rudimentary knowledge of the host language never lead to deep discussions, but the mere attempt to say a few words in the local tongue usually elicited appreciative smiles, be it in Athens, Antwerp, or Ancona.

I was reminded of my early linguistic efforts the other day when I found in my brother's house a booklet that helps the German traveler acquaint himself with idiomatic American. My brother spends several months each year in Florida and speaks English quite well. But he strives for perfection. Thus the book, whose title is, in translation, *The Peculiarities of Americans and their Language.* I immediately transferred it from his living room to the small room in the house where many people catch up on their reading while otherwise occupied, and informed myself intermittently about the peculiarities and the idiomatic expressions of the people among whom I live.

One peculiarity of Americans, so the book points out, is that they seldom ever close the doors of the rooms in which they sit and read or write. I remember that I also thought that was peculiar when I first landed here. To my astonishment, the book, however, concludes from this that Americans have a diminished sense of privacy. Another chapter, "How to react to a mugging," seems to suggest that any foreign tourist should expect to be robbed, and the book delivers the proper etiquette for that situation.

In the section on important idioms, the visitor learns how to carry on a casual conversation. Should you want to invite someone over to your apartment together with a few friends, the guide book suggests that you say nonchalantly: "Please come by my pad tonight. I am expecting a couple of cats." To avoid repetition, you might also propose: "Won't you come by to view the boob tube or to chew the fat tonight?" Dinner invitations are trickier. When invited, never forget to ask: "Are we dressing?" This, the book is careful to stress, poses the question if the dress is to be formal and not if it is a nudist party. Further, the idiomatic speaker, when asked if he enjoys the meal, is advised to respond: "Yummy, yummy!" If one has to turn down an invitation, the proper idiomatic response must be: "Oh, rats! I can't. Give me a rain check!" If in a conversation one can't remember a name, he is to assure the host that it is "on my tongue's tip." If asked about one's deceased parents, one is to say that "they keeled over" recently or that "they are pushing up the daisies." If the visitor wants to leave early, he is to explain his premature departure by pointing out that "a tempest is brewing."

The book also contains good advice for shoppers. It is, according to this guide, perfectly fine to let the salesperson know how much you want to spend and that "you don't want to pay through your nose." When entering the lingerie section, women are warned not to translate literally from German by referring to their "breast or bosom width," but to their "bust measure." Since sizes are numbered differently in America, the book helpfully hints that the Venus de Milo has a 48 bust measure. Now visualize the sculpture and decide if you want to go up or down.

My brother was puzzled that my reading sessions were accompanied by bursts of laughter. I explained that I have very few American friends who know how to speak idiomatically. But I do now, after reading the book.

November 27, 2002

∼

How do you say 'computer' in French? Very carefully

To the best of my knowledge, France is the only nation that sustains (since 1635) an official state-supported body, the Académie Française, whose main purpose it is to preserve the purity of the national language. And indeed, it seems that the French are in love with their language more than any other European nation. Even Americans have largely succumbed to the notion that French embodies amour, elegance, and charm whereas German stands for sauerkraut, sausage, and Walkyrie. Why would Americans think that way? Well, while Lafayette instructed the colonial ladies in the latest Parisian minuets, his Prussian colleague, von Steuben, drilled marching steps into the recruits. Perhaps that explains the bias.

However, even the French begin to have problems with impure injections into their beloved mother tongue. Globalization, and Americanization in particular, has invaded the French lexicon to a point that action beyond raising one's eyebrows appears mandatory. For years, purists have turned their noses up at words like 'weekend,' 'fax,' 'copyright,' 'rapper,' 'website,' 'airbag,' 'ketchup,' 'hamburger,' 'T-shirt,' 'cocktail,' or 'computer.' Many anglicisms are so deeply embedded in everyday French that purists speak disapprovingly of 'Franglais'—the unholy mixture of 'français' and 'anglais.' But this has not stopped the American linguistic tsunami triggered by U.S. pop culture, the electronics industry, and sports from flooding whole continents. Now the French are determined to build a dike.

Realizing that the forty sedate 'immortals' of the Académie Française might not act quickly and decisively enough to stem the American linguistic colonialization of their language, a group of vexed citizens started a political initiative with the goal of protecting the French language by law. And indeed, in 1994 the 'Loi Toubon,' named after the then minister of culture, Jacques Toubon, took effect. The Toubon Law imposes significant financial penalties for using a foreign language without French translation in advertisements, product labels, or even scholarly meetings.

An activist watchdog group, called 'Le droit de comprendre' (The Right to Understand), consisting largely of journalists, novelists, and language teachers and funded by the Ministry of Culture, now regularly screens department stores and billboards for products and advertisements that violate the xenophobic law. Any label marked 'Made in Taiwan' that does not have a French translation will be reported to the Chamber of Commerce. While brand names such as Ketchup and Kleenex are exempted and may be used in ads and displays, words like 'computer' may not; they are to be called 'ordinateurs,' a fax becomes a 'télécopie,' and popcorn 'maïs soufflé.' But terms like 'inflatable protective pillow'' (coussin gonflable de protection) for 'airbag' still resists broad acceptance. International ad campaigns with snappy slogans like "Do you yahoo?" or Nike's "Just do it!" have run into trouble with the language zealots because the Toubon Law demands that the French translation is printed exactly as large as the original advertisement text. Over 1,200 lawsuits have been brought so far against companies that allegedly violated the 'Loi Toubon.'

The latest victim of the French purifiers is Georgia Tech. The American university's overseas program in Lorraine instructs students from 22 different countries, only a third of them from France. The university's internet website was until recently only available in English, which brought the 'Right to Understand' watchdogs to the ramparts and landed Georgia Tech in court. Through several appeals the university argued that potential students surfing its web in Moscow, Milan, or Hamburg want to read the course descriptions in English and not in French only because the program happens to be located in France. In spite of long legal battles, the French judges never decided the issue and dismissed the suit over a technicality. Georgia Tech has meanwhile created and added a French page to its website. And the French in turn have created a word for 'web.' This will now be 'toile'—which in English means linen, cloth, canvas or, ahem, web.

The heirs of von Steuben, by the way, don't mind the linguistic globalization and, in good German, surf the web on the computer. However, it sounds so much more romantic to surf the toile on the ordinateur, n'est-ce pas?

June 21, 2000

~

Linguistic profiling: speaking while German

Recent years have brought us many reports about racial profiling, an alleged police practice of stopping citizens solely on the basis of their racial or ethnic characteristics. We hear complaints about the dangers of 'Driving while Black,' and more recently about the hazards of being investigated for 'Flying while Arab.' But after the recent attack on America, committed by nineteen young men, all of them fundamentalist Islamic Arabs, my guess is that airport security will probably not target as high security risks blond, blue-eyed Dutchmen and Jewish grandmothers from the Bronx. Undoubtedly profiles of potential hijackers will include ethnic characteristics, but with our capacity for linguistic sanitation, it will probably be given another name. I propose IPDRATWA, the Identification of People Determined to Redirect Air Traffic Without Authorization. That should be sensitive enough.

I never thought, of course, that one day I would myself become the victim of profiling—in my case linguistic profiling. I did not even know this form of discrimination existed but am pleased to note that I have attained victim status in at least one area. PBS ran a short feature some weeks ago showing that in telephone conversations many people can be identified as regards sex, race, age, ethnic origin, or social class. This fact then makes discrimination possible in job inquiries, rental applications, or requests for loans.

How am I a victim of linguistic profiling? In a recently published history of a big American university, I read that I was passed over for the presidency because I spoke with too much of an accent. I have long forgiven the search committee, because it is true: my speech immediately reveals my Germanic origins. This is to my advantage only around Holland, Michigan where most people assume that I am Dutch.

My colleagues in the university always knew my linguistic profile, too. I only needed to say 'hello' on the phone and immediately received the reply: "Good morning, Dr. Haenicke." Based on this easy linguistic identification, my wife jokingly exhorted me to refrain from making obscene phone calls. I never made such calls, but only because I completely lacked interest in this unusual form of communication, not out of fear of detection. Cross my heart!

But I know at least one person who lets her accent work in her favor. Luche Query, the Puerto Rican-born wife of one of our former university deans, successfully fought off telemarketers, fundraisers, and similar telephone pests by identifying herself as the Query's maid. With her beautiful Spanish accent she could work the linguistic stereotype to her advantage every time.

Worse than one person speaking with an accent is, of course, a conversation between two accent-afflicted interlocutors. I was once engaged in a conversation with Henry Kissinger at a party when everyone around us fell silent. This was, unfortunately, not because of the intellectual depth of our remarks. The other guests found it hilarious hearing two immigrants hacking away with their loud, thick German accents. To avoid comparisons to Colonel Klink, we quickly switched to German, which we both speak free of any foreign accent.

For at least one student, my accent led to severe frustration. At Ohio State we had a large number of math classes taught by Asian graduate students whose accented English was quite unfamiliar to the ears of kids from isolated farms outside of Chilicothe or Wapakoneta. One of these students, approaching a failing grade in a math course, decided to complain about his instructor's unintelligible Japanese accent to the dean, at that time a mathematician from Oxford, England. The dean's crisp, clipped English was equally traumatic for the student; so he decided to come to the highest academic authority, the provost, to unload his grievance. He sat down in my office, where I greeted him with friendly words. He looked in disbelief at me, his third linguistic disaster, and exclaimed: "I can't understand a word my instructor says. It wasn't much better with the dean. And now I see that you don't speak no good English neither." Ever since, I know for sure that not everyone in this country celebrates diversity.

November 14, 2001

∽

III. As I see it:
Observations, Opinions, and Anecdotes

The definition of 'old' changes with age

Young people don't waste much time thinking about growing old. Why should they? Children and even young men and women have only a limited concept of what it means to cross those magic lines separating youth, middle age, and old age.

If I were asked at what age these transitions occur, I would be hard pressed. When flower children and hippies ruled, they warned us not to trust anyone over thirty. Is that the magic threshold between youth and middle age? And then at fifty, does one step into old age? Or is it sixty? Are there three stages, each about thirty years long, that segment our lives?

I think it all depends on perspective. From my early teens I distinctly remember 'old man' Schmeissing, a local policeman in our little town, who several times chased me on foot and who was fast enough, in spite of his 'old man' status, to make my escapes very narrow ones. He was perhaps forty, but definitely, in the eyes of a thirteen-year old boy, as old as Methuselah.

Later, when I was selecting a thesis advisor for my doctoral dissertation, I seriously questioned if my favorite professor would last long enough to oversee the three-year endeavor. I was twenty-five; he was sixty-five—an unimaginable age difference of forty years. Such are the follies of youth.

Nowadays, having passed that second threshold into the sixties, I see the situation quite differently. Surprisingly, I don't feel 'old.' Granted, I don't sleep anymore like a baby; my bones get creaky occasionally; and nature has seen fit to send me to my cardiologist, Ben Perry, more often than to my barber, Jerry Brown—but I simply won't admit to feeling like an old man.

I tell myself that it is because I don't 'think old,' that I remain curious about new ideas, trends, books, concepts, and developments. Neither do I look at most of my contemporaries as old.

Their hair may seem grayer than a decade ago, but their conversations continue to be engaging, lively, and young. And there is always Grecian Formula.

As one gets older, for reasons of self-respect, self-preservation, or sheer defiance, one adopts the concept that 'old' is more an attitudinal than a biological state. And indeed, I have met old people who were only in their thirties. I occasionally welcomed new professors decades my junior who did not 'think young.' I recall particularly well a young man, barely thirty, who endured my sermon on the university's expectations. When I asked if he had any questions, I expected a discussion on library resources, research support, and future challenges. But he showed interest only in the university retirement system. We had hired an old man. Pity the students.

While senior citizens may see themselves as 'not old,' young people have a different perspective. I notice it with my students, typically nineteen to twenty-four year olds, who each year tend to look younger. They may realize that I am not quite over the hill because I can still teach them a thing or two, but when it comes to my biological age they are as overwhelmed as I probably would have been in younger years.

A while ago, during a seminar, a student gave a presentation on a literary journal that ceased publication at the end of World War I. As a literary scholar I was, of course, very familiar with that journal. Therefore the student assumed that I had been a reader of that publication in my youth, and she said so. I told her that was impossible since I had been born in 1935. Still I could see her reaching back to the Middle Ages and figuring out my age. An expression of disbelief crossed her face. "Wow!" she said and then added: "Do you still drive your own car?"

Yes, I do. And I also still buy green bananas.

March 15, 2000

∾

Hanging on to dignity and dear life in an open hospital gown

Much to my regret, I can claim considerable expertise as a patient. Over the last twenty years, I was hospitalized twelve times in six different hospitals in the U.S. and Germany. My last hospital stay had striking similarities with previous experiences. There are basic repetitive patterns.

Entering as an emergency patient, my first objective is always to hang on to dear life, immediately followed by the attempt to hang on to my dignity, an almost equally difficult task. I am immediately stripped to the essential me, laid bare as in my first hour on earth. Someone attaches a plastic banderole around my left wrist, which always makes me feel like a carrier pigeon. Next, I am tethered by plastic tubes and cords to monitors and IV poles, restricting every move. Should I have had coffee or any other bladder stimulating liquids before my arrival, additional moments of embarrassment will quickly and surely ensue. To preserve my personal dignity in such a moment is hard work.

If an X-ray is required, a photographic plate, which has just been removed from the hospital freezer, is put behind my bare back. Often this flash of ice on the spine is enough to jolt me back to consciousness.

Thereafter, the hospital gown. It is the great leveler. Everybody looks equally destitute and impoverished in that garment. It is designed to reduce the patient's sense of individuality to an absolute minimum and his sense of shame and privacy to nil. The back of the gown opens generously, in cases of obese patients it opens widely, displaying quite undesirable vistas. This may be another strategy to cut hospital costs because the various rear views are distinct appetite suppressants.

Then follows the plastic phase. One eats and drinks from plastic plates and cups, sits on plastic chairs, and sleeps doused with sweat on plastic mattresses and pillow covers. One is surrounded by all the long forgotten comforts of motels from the fifties. Whether or not one is leaking in the area, one's middle section rests on a 'pink pad,' placed there to "prevent any problems, you know."

And there are linguistic peculiarities. The pronoun 'we' is used in phrases like: "How did WE sleep last night?" This makes me feel like a lover awakening after a night of delight, but with total amnesia. Did WE really sleep together? When I request to use the bathroom, the young nurse says: "Why don't WE use the bedside commode?" WE? I then suggest that she go first. But such attempts at humor are always lost.

And the biorhythm of patients and staff differs vastly. After a sleeping pill has been administered at midnight, someone wakes me at 4 a.m. to weigh me. "Just step out of your bed for a moment, and then I'll let you get right back to sleep." For Pete's sake! It takes me a long time to go back to sleep, just long enough to be awakened forty minutes later by someone who stocks my linen closet at 4:45 a.m.

How to overcome the indignities connected with being sick and sleeping in ugly gowns on plastic mattresses? I prevailed this past week because of the outstanding care. Being in the hands of two top-flight physicians, Ben Perry and Tim Fischell; and having Rachel Koelsch, the young resident physician, lighting up my room every morning; seeing nothing but caring smiles, helpfulness, and kindness from the nurses and aides on the floor made me forget all temporary hardship. They were a wonderful team, and I thank all of them deeply.

They know me only in my drafty hospital gown shuffling up and down the corridor. But one day, after the pigeon banderole is removed and when all the hematomas, bruises, and puncture wounds inflicted on me have faded, I will visit them in my best Sunday suit and show them what I really look like. None of them will recognize me.

March 29, 2000

∼

It's fun savoring 'Schadenfreude' in balmy Florida

There are, in any language, words that defy literal translation, and approximations must suffice. So it is with the German word

'Gemütlichkeit,' of which the Germans are very proud and which they consider essentially and inimitably German. The word conveys an atmosphere of homespun, sentimental coziness, congenial fellowship, and lightheartedness all woven together.

While there may be considerable pride in the German atmosphere of Gemütlichkeit, no such feeling should exist about another untranslatable German word: 'Schadenfreude.' I am not convinced that this word expresses yet another purely German sentiment, since everyone in the world knows the feeling, although English knows no exact equivalent for it.

Schadenfreude is the feeling of glee and secret delight over someone else's bad luck and misery. The feeling registers more strongly if the star-crossed person is one's competitor at the office or in business, but it can extend, under the right circumstances, to good neighbors or members of one's own family. One thoroughly enjoys, without necessarily expressing it verbally, the fact that someone else has a hard time while all is going well for oneself. Every honest person, I am sure, will admit to having felt Schadenfreude sometime in his life. What a despicable attitude, but oh! how sweet it is!

As I type this, I am vacationing for a few weeks in Florida, and the word Schadenfreude comes to mind in practically every conversation I have with other Michiganders whom I meet on my outings into Naples and Ft. Myers where many of them winter. The locals call Northerners 'snowbirds' because of their annual migration to the South where Floridians welcome their purchasing power but threaten, with bumper sticker messages: "When I am old, I'll move up North and drive slowly."

The snowbirds' delight over other people's bad luck and misery centers essentially on the weather. A typical snowbird will take personal credit for the warm temperatures and ample sunshine. After all, why not?! Didn't he have the good sense to retire and buy or rent property in the sun? Isn't it just self-inflicted injury to work for a living up North and to suffer cold and snow and fight icy roads each winter?

Out of habit, and since there is little else to do, many snowbirds begin the day accumulating weather information. Not about their own local Florida weather—that is fairly predictable and uninteresting. They want information about the weather back home. The worse the news, the better. The more snow predicted for the home town, the deeper the drop in wind chill factors up North, the more icy the hardship that visits his neighbor—the more enjoyable the day for the Florida snowbird. What a good feeling to sit sparsely clad at the pool, pick up the phone and call home and inquire, quite innocently: "How is the weather up there?"

This question, of course, is not asked in order to receive information or to verify the weather forecast and the gruesome TV pictures of blizzards, stalled cars, and delayed airplanes. The question is asked out of pure Schadenfreude, because the answer, "The weather here is terrible," is already known in advance and gleefully expected. The snowbird's response: "I am sorry to hear that. Isn't that too bad!" is taken for what it is: disingenuous and full of Schadenfreude. This brief and ritual beginning of each snowbird/non-snowbird telephone conversation makes the snowbird's day.

But Schadenfreude works both ways. Nothing upsets the snowbird more than to learn that the weather back home is just fine. Descriptions of a mild, sunny, and beautiful winter day in Michigan irritate the snowbird to no end. No ice on the roads, no cars in ditches, no reports from exhausted snow-shoveling neighbors—that's a real bummer for the snowbird. Terrible those occasional days in January when Florida temperatures drop to near freezing levels similar to those in Michigan. On days like these no phone calls to the North are placed by the snowbird. Bereft of his own Schadenfreude, he may even avoid receiving calls from back home in order to rob his Michigan friends from expressing their own glee over the mild Michigan weather.

But, in the end, Michigan winters being what they are, the snowbird usually wins the contest over whose Schadenfreude is more frequent and more intense. As usual, Florida this year has just wonderful weather. And with gleeful feelings about my own good fortune and my Kalamazoo friends' bad luck, I put the laptop aside and dive back into the pool.

February 17, 1999

≈

How would you like your dog?

A German proverb says: "Andre Länder, andre Sitten," which means, freely translated, other countries have different customs and habits, so don't travel the world and expect people to behave exactly as you would in your own country. It is a good mindset with which to travel because some of the customs in other lands are quite astonishing. I am offering here some recent observations on the status of animals, particularly dogs, in the social life of nations.

Dogs play entirely different roles depending on whether one travels in parts of Asia or parts of Europe. In northern Europe one finds the dog usually *under* the table; in Bavaria the dog occasionally sits *at* the table; in other parts of the world the dog is *on* the table, and I mean right on the plate, cooked and deboned.

Of all the uses of this widely beloved pet, dog as a culinary object has the least appeal to me personally. I say this knowing full well that the multi-culturalists will probably chide me for not 'celebrating' diversity of cuisine. But somewhere I draw the line. Dog is definitely one diversity barbecue that must be celebrated without me.

However, I cannot be quite certain that I have never indulged in dog as a delicacy. Several of my hosts in Asia, when questioned, would not reveal what was being served while they exchanged knowing smiles among themselves. "Try it, you'll like it," they promised. There were some dishes that had the texture of things I had never eaten before; so who knows? But perhaps it was only snake, another treat that I would not put on my list of favorite snacks.

While I do not like dogs, howsoever prepared, *on* the table, I have become accustomed to having them sit *under* the table. In Germany, I once had a meal with my friend Greg Dobson in the elegant dining room of Spangenberg castle. A stylishly clad couple sat close by. We thoroughly enjoyed the refined atmosphere and the exceptional service of the fine restaurant. However, throughout the lunch we heard occasional grunting and belching from the next table and interpreted the unappetizing sounds as the other guests' approval of the chef's culinary artistry. Other countries, other customs, so we surmised. However, when the couple left, out from under the table appeared a St. Bernard-sized dog who walked with solemn dignity behind its owners to the exit.

I can't remember ever having shared a restaurant dining room with a dog in the U.S., not even in a modest establishment. Health regulations probably prevent the presence of animals where food is being served to the public.

But Germans, I am sure, would not hear of any such restrictions. Particularly in Bavaria dogs seem to have rights that equal those of humans, and many dogs deserve such rights since they usually behave as well and occasionally even better than their owners. Any Munich Biergarten has on display man and dog, peacefully seated side by side, combating their thirst—and while its master broodingly stares into his beer, Waldi laps up some water from a bowl. I am convinced that many Germans could not think of a better companion to have a drink or a meal with than their dog.

My wife had her own dog encounter in a Munich streetcar that she cannot forget. She was standing on the back platform of the tram minding her own business when an elderly lady entered leading a rather large dog on a leash. Immediately the dog started barking and snapping at Carol who retreated in fright. The old lady became quite cross at my wife and accused her of upsetting her dog. Why else would the poor creature bark? None of the other passengers saw anything wrong with that Bavarian line of reasoning. Carol moved to the front of the streetcar.

Perhaps not in Asia, but in Bavaria the dog always wins.

August 25, 1999

~

New Year's resolution number one: lose weight!

If I were a betting man, I would wager that most New Year's resolutions start with: Lose weight! And that usually includes the resolution to exercise more. Whoever puts those two resolutions on a list is smart and should heed them. They save lives; they make one feel better; and thus make eminently good sense.

And that is about as much Pollyanna talk as I will dispense on this topic. For I must add: for some of us, they are also the hardest resolutions to follow. Witness the fact that they show up on the same list year after year, and usually written again and again by the same people.

I know what I am talking about. My relationship with food can only be classified as a fatal attraction. For many years, I used to buy food that tasted good. Now I buy only food that is good for me—which is not the same thing by a long shot.

I have learned to fake disgust with many items that I remember with fondness: beautifully marbled steaks, sour cream, juicy pork chops, coconut sprinkled truffles, half and half, butter, lox, ripe Camembert or rich Stilton cheeses, and other such utter calorie-laden obscenities. Each walk through the aisles of a food store turns into a trip down memory lane, a sentimental journey during which the sins and excesses of my younger years blend into one beautiful, albeit remorsefully remembered, past.

Nowadays, after numerous fortifying lectures by dieticians, I am conditioned to steer through the strong currents of temptation to those islands of health and virtue in each food store where artificial creamers and artificial bacon, fat-free bologna, fat-free cheeses, ultra-lean turkey meat, eggbeaters, Nutrasweet, and skim milk await the dieting and health-oriented customer.

In the old days, entering the store with a lustful appetite seemed sufficient. Now, a master's degree in chemistry with a minor in food science are almost a *sine qua non* for all who want to make informed decisions about heart-healthy food purchases. A great deal of reading is required before an item is allowed in the shopping cart. Each package indicates the percentage of saturated and unsaturated fat contained in a serving, the milligrams of sugar and sodium, the number of calories in each one-ounce bite, the total carbohydrates, the amount of cholesterol, and assorted additional chemical information. Often, after reading the entire label of, let's say fat-free cheese, one wonders if the cheese originated in a lab cauldron or in a cow. If the taste of the product were the only clue, the lab cauldron would have it.

But even here mind triumphs over matter and taste. Once one is sufficiently brain-washed to believe that salt-free food actually tastes better "because salt hides rather than enhances the natural taste," one is also ready to accept that the taste of artificial ham and eggbeaters is superior to the original. Very few health conscious persons ever reach that level of absolute self-deception. I envy them. To accept the artificial taste of artificial products, I use the standard method. One must stop eating real eggs and real ham for about a year, or until one has completely forgotten how they are supposed to taste. Then one begins to eat the cholesterol-free fake products and behold: the deception takes hold and takes over.

With time, one begins to believe that ham is *supposed* to taste like an amalgam of shoe leather and stale bread. With even more time, most people develop an almost religious feeling of virtuousness about their rejection of red meat, French fries, and real cheeses. Some even develop a missionary's zeal about converting the infidels who still pursue with unabashed gusto the forbidden fat-laden delicacies.

So once again I start my list of New Year's resolutions with the old challenge. But as I stroll down the aisles at D&W, I look into the shelves at many old friends and mumble: "Thanks for the memories."

January 5, 2000

~

Do children or do parents compete at the science fair?

When visiting exhibitions of children's paintings, I am always taken by the strong imagination displayed by the fledgling painters who obviously created their art without adult intervention. An adult steering the child into painting 'correctly' would take much of the naïve charm away from the effort.

However, at science fairs in which third and fourth graders display their projects, I sometimes suspect that I am viewing the combined skills of clans rather than those of elementary school children. And when it comes to technical school projects, the expertise of families is often pooled, with little Bobby providing little more than the seminal idea. Anyone with children has been there. I certainly have. In fact, several of my parental failures and triumphs stem from such projects, and the memories haunt or delight me, as the case may be.

My first abysmal failure occurred when my son, then a Cub Scout, entered a competition for which each boy had to build a car, 12 to 15 inches long and not weighing more than a pound, that would roll down a ten-foot ramp. The scoutmaster instructed parents to help by "providing materials found in every household and to supervise the proper use of tools necessary for the construction."

In our family, father and son had never constructed anything but paper airplanes in summer and paper garlands at Christmas, and no masculine bonding in the tool shop had occurred, mainly because we did not have one. All we had was a tiny workbench with a vise and assorted saws, hammers, nails, and other 'materials found in every home.' So Kurt hammered and sawed and painted away under my inexpert guidance, and finally produced a klotzy chunk of a car that would indeed roll slowly down a ramp, if given a good push. It looked like something an eight-year-old would build, and with satisfaction on our faces we faced the competition.

As we carried our little monstrosity into the hall, proud fathers and sons were lined up with car models that could easily have been accepted at the annual Automobile Show downtown. We had not realized that 'materials found in every household' included wind tunnels, kilns, professional design equipment, and the like. We had also forgotten that we lived in Detroit, the Motor City, where every second father worked for either Ford, GM, Chrysler, or one of its many suppliers. The expert skills of experienced engineers had been brought into the race, and our pathetic but honest entry was no match for the sleek and perfectly aerodynamic jewels that had originated in professional engineering and design studios.

We came in second to last. Only one fatherless boy, whose car lost three wheels as it tumbled aimlessly down the ramp, came in lower than we. The winning boy bathed in the glory of 'his' car that he clearly had not built himself.

Kurt's next project was to build a rocket. As provost of a large research university, I toyed with the temptation of unleashing our fine engineering college and its vast tool shops on the next 'children's competition.' Surely our professors could 'supervise' my son in building a rocket that would knock the socks off the competition. But I realized what a bad lesson my son would learn by winning this way.

Our only father-son triumph came when we won second prize in the school bake sale, fair and square. Without compromising our integrity, my son measured and mixed the ingredients, filled them into a form and baked a prize-winning cake—all under fatherly supervision and with materials found in every household. He could honestly claim that he had made it himself.

My son became neither an engineer nor a baker. He is a writer. Now, if his metaphors don't soar like rockets, or if the wheels should come off his sentences, he does not blame his father. He knows that he can only be proud of a project if it truly is his own.

March 22, 2000

∼

On age-spot removers and bibs for seniors

I entered seniordom several years ago, when a very young girl at the D&W check-out counter looked at me with the taxing eyes of an appraiser and then inquired if I was a senior. I was totally unprepared for that question. I presided at the time over a large university and felt full to the brim with energy. But her question was not impolite. On that particular day senior shoppers were receiving a storewide 10% discount on their purchases, and she wanted to ascertain if I qualified.

I have always loved a good discount. So I threw my concerns regarding privacy to the wind and inquired at what age a person becomes a senior. At 55, 60, or 65? Does one have to be retired? She was not sure. But I could read her mind. It told her that senior status is reached a few years before people started looking like me. When I told her I was sixty, she audibly gasped and immediately rang up the discount. In the eyes of teenagers—and I have seen it in their eyes many times since—a man of sixty is right up there with the biblical patriarchs and close to a wheelchair and incontinence.

It was a life-changing experience. Ever since that day, I ask for senior discounts whenever I open my wallet. The local movie houses reduce my ticket by a few dimes; selected restaurants shave off a dollar or two by serving me senior portions on smaller plates; the video store has my senior status logged in to its computer and automatically reduces my bill; the Kalamazoo Institute of Arts sports special senior donor categories; certain 'participating' hotels let me sleep for a few bucks less; airlines are deducting from my fare an amount equal to two bags of peanuts; and the national parks service allows me to peek into the Grand Canyon for $5 less than the young father with a family of five standing next to me.

It often occurs to me that the young father raising four kids might probably need the discount more than I. In fact, many of my contemporaries in the discount brigade are by no means impecunious. They travel extensively to exotic locations; they lavish gifts on their children and grandchildren; they drive expensive cars; and they donate generously to local charities. But they love that senior discount and wallow in delight each time the usually minuscule deduction appears on their check. It is the only tangible benefit of seniorhood.

In my more philosophical moments, I view the senior discount as life's attempt to recompense us for the many distinct shortcomings of old age. But when I consider all the inconveniences and exasperation that accompany advancing age, I must conclude that a 10% discount in return is neither fair nor sufficient.

The fact that national data banks now identify me as a senior has activated the mail order industry, which peppers me with catalogs offering items presumably of special appeal to people my age. There is the Tai Chi course for seniors promising the participating grandpa the "flexibility of a child, the vitality of a lumberjack, and the wisdom of a sage." A California company wants to sell me its "Age Spot Fade Cream," which makes its user look 30 years younger. Magnifying glasses are advertised for reading the telephone book accompanied by a phone with triple-sized numbers. Then there is the portable urinal, "a godsend when restrooms aren't near," combined with the sharply reduced "Incontinence-related Rash Protectant Cream."

I am not ready for any of this yet, thank heavens! So far, I am keeping only the ad for the Cotton Terry Bib, reduced for seniors from twelve to six dollars, which, the ad promises, "gets you the protection you need and keeps you dry and comfortable during every meal. Generous size extends to your lap for total coverage while eating." I have often longed for this item while eating spaghetti. The people who clean my ties probably think I should have bought the bib thirty years ago. But I do wonder what our local restaurateurs would say if I showed up with this senior protection tool, giving myself total coverage while eating my senior portion. I guess I'll find out eventually.

January 8, 2003

∾

Name that Taiwanese city on the East China Sea

Some people equate doing crossword puzzles with intellectual prowess. During the nineties, rumors abounded that Bill Clinton could do the Sunday *New York Times* crossword puzzle, notorious for its complexity, in twenty minutes or less, and it was further rumored that he did it in ink. That is, of course, the epitome of mental acuity and confidence, since pencil and eraser are the more typical tools of the puzzle enthusiast. I never tried to emulate this or the more carnal of Bill Clinton's favorite pastimes, mainly out of fear that I might end up in a pool of blood, as my wife is simply not insightful enough to recognize a broad right-wing conspiracy when she sees one.

But when it comes to doing crossword puzzles, my wife is a true aficionado. She gets it from her late mother, who measured her life by the intervals between the appearance of certain crossword puzzles, her favorite being the one in the *Boston Globe* weekend edition. She had convinced herself that entering little letters into little boxes kept Alzheimer's at bay, and she solved crossword puzzles with the tenacity of a devoted researcher. Family members could not enter her house without being quizzed about areas of expertise germane to their profession, gender, or age. My son-in-law's brain was picked for information about sports figures and popular culture; my daughter delivered names of minor actors based on her vast knowledge of the sit-com industry; and my wife, a former reference librarian, was expected to act as the resident expert on all other trivia. I was less seldom accosted by my mother-in-law since my pronounced aversion to this odd sideline of intellectual activity is well known in the family.

However, my wife devotedly carries on the crossword puzzle tradition established by her mother. I don't think she engages in this sport to keep her mental agility; she just enjoys figuring out all kinds of puzzles. Not unlike her mother, she has carefully developed a network of informants, mainly relatives, who feed her bits of intelligence from areas in which she is less competent, such as TV personalities, baseball statistics, the church fathers, the stops on the Trans-Siberian railroad, rap lyrics, or animal life in the Amazon. Her puzzle passion also may explain the presence of an unusually large collection of encyclopedias and dictionaries in our house, but also of reference books that cover history, music, art, religion, literature, finance, science, the law, and more. For the solver of crossword puzzles must be a polymath, a person of deep and vast learning, since the questions that arise weekly from the *Boston Globe* far transcend the knowledge of a conventionally educated person like me. I would never know that an ancient city of Canaan northwest of Jerusalem—five letters and ending in 'r'—is Gezer; nor could I tell her that the Taiwanese city on the East China Sea—seven letters, the fourth and the fifth being 'l' and 'u'—is, of course, Keelung. Even my usually reliable knowledge of history is challenged when I can't come up with the name of the architect of the White House (James Hoban).

The spouse of the crossword puzzler is never ever safe from unexpected interrogation. Lying in bed, I am absorbed in reading a novel about the life of Confucius, but my bedmate needs to know who won the Nobel prize in physics in 1922 (four letters), the name of a Verdi opera ending with an 'o,' and a Latin expression beginning with 'ip' and ending in 'it.' But after I reluctantly reveal the information (Bohr, Otello, *ipse dixit),* the mental excursion into modern science, opera, and antiquity make it difficult to find the way back to the Chinese master on the banks of the Yellow River.

Not being a crossworder, I sometimes wonder. How will I keep my mind sharp and flexible as I embark on the pending trip from being an elderly person to being really old? Not having the names of African nations, medieval discoverers, and rap singers constantly on the tip of my tongue, will I end up sitting in Bronson Park mindlessly feeding the pigeons? I really worry about it.

November 13, 2002

∾

Observations on fashion codes in health clubs

The increased frequency of my visits to the new Bronson Athletic Club is not the result of delayed New Year's resolutions. Rather, two major forces combined in pushing me onto the path to improved health: the stern admonitions of my cardiologist, Ben Perry, and my wife's raised eyebrows whenever I dismount the bathroom scales. I am comforted by the thought that my cardiologist would rather see me in his office than mumble, "I told you so" at my funeral, and that my wife, after four decades of marriage, still wishes to extend our years of happy companionship.

With these good thoughts in mind, thrice a week I don my exercise apparel— sweatpants and an old T-shirt. I never liked the word 'sweatpants.' Something unappealingly odiferous is connected with that designation. Besides, my exercise level never reaches the intensity that triggers the excretions which give these pants their appalling name. But at the health club one cannot arrive in nicely pleated pants and a neat white shirt. Health clubs and insiders on the exercise scene have their own fashion code that wants to be respected. Just to occupy my mind during sit-ups, I have collected a few pertinent observations.

The proper fashion look in athletic clubs is distinctly on the grubby side. Socks with holes attesting to heroically run marathons, and shirts with tears produced by bulging, rippling muscles are displayed like badges of honor. If shorts are worn, make sure that your underwear does not match their color and protrudes a few inches below them. Such are the fashion dictates of the health scene.

In each athletic club, generally speaking, I observe two different kinds of users. There are the lords of the realm, tanned, trim, muscled, and who show no discernible body fat. They walk with bouncing steps, strutting their stuff in tight-fitting clothes or minimalist textiles. One wonders what the heck they are doing in a health club, looking like perfect specimens in no need of any physical upgrades. Stepping up to any exercise machine, they set its weight or resistance level breathtakingly high and begin to push or lift. With occasional grunts they admit that their Herculean strength has its borders, but even after the final primordial scream they still do two or three more pushes, each one a triumph of muscle over machine. When these high level exercisers are done, one realizes that the word 'sweat' as in sweatpants and sweatshirts is appropriate and descriptive.

The second group are club members who wear loose-fitting, tent-like clothes that hang generously around their limbs. These garments are not designed to proudly reveal their owners' eye-catching physiques. Their purpose is rather to camouflage their wearers' unsightly bulges or atrophied leg, arm, and chest muscles. I belong, and am sorry to admit it, to the group with the loose-fitting duds, which, in my case, conceal both bulge and atrophy, depending on the body parts. We exercisers of the lower order set the weights on machines at moderate levels, so low in fact that many of us, when we leave the exercise station, re-adjust the weight level upwards so that the next user will not burst into laughter over the pathetic level of our best efforts.

Only in one club location no fashion code prevails, and all attire is reduced to a white towel. This is the locker room, the great equalizer. I never got quite accustomed to the complete lack of inhibition which most American men exhibit when they enter and leave the showers. The physical disparity between high and low level exercisers becomes even more pronounced in the locker room. But here, even gargantuan figures, otherwise only seen in Rubens paintings, unashamedly parade around with a naked innocence last known in paradise. My academic colleague, Ed Edwards, an athlete and locker room expert, once taught me proper locker room etiquette: don't shake hands; look the other person firmly in the eye; and never let your eyes roam below shoulder level. That way all comparative observations about differing fashions in birthday suits can be avoided.

May 29, 2002

∾

Do hookers have hearts of gold?

Teaching is said to be the world's second oldest profession. I questioned this when recently I read an unusual report from Greece. There, a member of the so-called oldest profession was memorialized as a gifted teacher who had conveyed the secret delights of her horizontal trade to many generations of young men. When the prostitute Amalia (73) died in Thessaloniki without relatives, her grateful neighbors, mainly men, petitioned the city government to hand over her remains to them for a proper and loving funeral. "She was for many of us our first teacher. She was good, full of love, and when we had no money, she did not demand any. Now we want to do something for her, even if late," a male neighbor commented on Greek television, being careful to cover his face with his hands. Her student-customers eventually organized a beautiful funeral that was attended by many well-known personalities from local business and politics.

It is touching to see such devotion to a former teacher. Should I be envious, realizing that her hands-on teaching style undoubtedly drew more undivided attention from her students than my academic lectures? Not really. After all, Amalia was expertly at home in two of the oldest professions—something with which a mere literature professor cannot compete.

As Americans, we tend to see prostitution differently. I doubt that anyone here would recognize in its practice an element of

103

teaching, although it may be present in some cases. The famous actor James Earl Jones, who grew up in Northern Michigan, describes in his autobiography how a covered wagon, hiding one or more ladies of the night, periodically stopped in his rural community. Fathers and uncles, either unwilling or perhaps too embarrassed to deliver the customary 'birds and the bees' talk, would instead heave the pubescent boys into the dark wagon from which they emerged again after fifteen minutes, wide-eyed and breathless, but now fundamentally knowledgeable in the ways of the flesh.

Not in everyday life, but in the movies we often romanticize prostitution. Who doesn't remember *Gone with the Wind* where Rhett Butler's friend, the noble and generous local madam, saves a whole group of Southern gentlemen by providing a false bordello alibi for them? And then there are the incomparable Shirley McLaine in *Irma La Douce* and the glamorous Julia Roberts in *Pretty Woman*, two hookers with hearts of gold.

I harbored sweet notions of hookers myself once. In our town older men, leaning over the bar, used to remark with a gleam in their eyes: "When I die, I want to die like Dr. Bimmermann." What kind of desirable death had the good doctor met? A local dentist, widowed in his best years, Dr. Bimmermann, each Wednesday afternoon, took the train to the next big city where, according to rumor, he experienced cardiac arrest during an amorous embrace in a brothel. In America, doctors play golf on Wednesday afternoon.

As one would expect, the Germans are more practical and organized in their approach to prostitution. The country's estimated 400,000 sex workers (not prostitutes, please!) who serve 1.2 Million customers per day will now have, because of a bill passed in parliament, legal standing and the right to claim social security, health insurance, and a pension for their potentially arduous work. They also have the right to sue in court (small claims, I assume) customers who refuse to pay, and they may openly discriminate by turning would-be-customers away.

Moreover, some Germans have always recognized that there are evils far worse than prostitution. In my student days in Catholic Bavaria we told the following anecdote: The father comes home and says to his wife: "Mother, I have bad news. Our son has just told me that he is going to marry a prostitute." The mother blanches, makes three signs of the cross, and faints. As she awakes, she cries: "I can't believe it. Tell me it isn't so." But the father repeats the news once again, whereupon the mother miraculously recovers and exclaims: "Praised be the Lord! The first time you spoke I thought you said he wanted to marry a Protestant."

January 30, 2002

~

Revisiting books of youth may lead to a rediscovery of self

One of the great luxuries which I currently enjoy is having time to read for pleasure. For over twenty-five years, I held academic positions which forced me, day in and day out, to peruse financial statements, office memos, funding requests, general office correspondence, or accreditation reports. Although their respective authors undoubtedly put great effort into these communications to the president, none remain memorable or trigger the wish to re-read them. These days I read exclusively what I want to read, not what I must read, and the treasure trove of history, biography, poetry, and novels again lies open before me.

All my life, I have been an avid reader. I was very fortunate to have friends in my teens who also loved to read and with whom I could exchange and discuss books which fascinated and enthused us. Most of the books I read when I was fifteen or sixteen, I remember vividly to this day and also some of the long debates I had about them with my friends at the time.

Occasionally now, I take some of those books off the shelf and read them again, fifty years later. It is a wonderful experience that I highly recommend. A few books we read many times during our lives, and they become steady and trusted companions. But it is a powerful experience going back to books that defined our youth and that we have not read in between.

I always found it intriguing that books I loved could make less of an impression on other readers. We can fail a book, or a book can fail us—depending on the care with which the reading is done; the mood in which the readers find themselves while reading; or the emotional or intellectual experiences readers bring to the book. The dissimilar impact on *different readers* is easy to explain.

It is similarly easy to explain the changed impact of a book on *the same reader* at a later time in his life. After all, it should not come as a surprise that a lifetime of experience mightily changes a book's impact. But the great pleasure of reacquainting myself with a book of my youth lies not only in noting its changed impact; it also has other benefits. The greatest is the miracle of encountering oneself again, the youthful reader of half a century ago, and the rediscovery of the fanciful dreams and uncertain emotions of one's earlier self. With fondness and nostalgia I remember the particular features of the books that occupied and overwhelmed me then. When I was twelve, for instance, I fantasized about slipping into the heroic role of Edmond Dantes, *The Count of Monte-Christo.* A few years later, I sensed for the first time deep anger and indignation about harsh social conditions while reading Charles Dickens; was incensed at the religious persecution depicted in Werfel's *The Forty Days of Musa Dagh;* and at fifteen, with great curiosity and still well-remembered ambiguous and tentative feelings, I read countless times the love scenes between the courageous Robert Jordan and the fascinating and beautiful Maria in Hemingway's *For Whom The Bell Tolls.*

Most of us read for content in our youth—not for style, composition, or other artistic elements. The story mattered most. What happened and how it ended drove our interest. But along with the love of reading, an appreciation grew for how a story was presented, in what way it was told, and how the language flowed. Thus the reading for content, powerful in itself, developed into a much deeper involvement and enjoyment that characterizes the adult reader.

Revisiting the favorite books of my youth, I also gratefully remember all the people who read to me as a child, who taught and encouraged me to read, who gave me my first books and thus opened wide the doors to the limitless world of knowledge and enjoyment. A belated blessing on each and every one of them! Would that every child could enter the world of reading as happily as I did.

January 3, 2001

∾

I remember your name perfectly, but...

"I remember your name perfectly, but I just can't think of your face," is one of many famous spoonerisms. I envy those lucky people who unfailingly remember names, even of persons to whom they were introduced only briefly and a long time ago. Politicians often have this uncanny memory, a powerful tool in public relations. After I became president of WMU, I had been introduced to the governor and I chatted with him for about ten minutes. Months later, sitting in a hotel in Washington, D.C., Jim Blanchard strolled in, crossed the vast lobby and greeted me with the correct first and last name— in my case a double challenge. I was flattered and enormously impressed.

I, on the other hand, struggle to remember names, particularly when I meet a familiar person in an unfamiliar context. When I began my work at Ohio State, I was quickly introduced to several hundred faculty members and staff. I did my best to remember names and match them with faces. One night, I was out for dinner with my wife when a gentleman greeted us from his table across the restaurant. I recognized the face instantly; in fact, I knew that I had talked to the man just recently. Obviously a member of the faculty. But who? A physics professor? A historian? A dean? Finally, I went over to his table to exchange a few collegial words about the university. However, the moment I shook his hand, I remembered how I knew him. He was the service man who had repaired our furnace a few weeks earlier.

We expect people to recall our names, and when they do, we take this as a sign of personal respect. Every Bob who is addressed as Richard resents it. Even if we have difficult foreign names, we cringe when we see our names misspelled. Every time I write to my friend Carol Waszkiewicz, I go back to my address book to check. Just in case. In this country where foreign names are legion, one meets frequent challenges. Are Ananthan Venkatachalam and Ter Chong Wang male or female? If I correspond with them, I go to great lengths to find out. I myself don't respond to the frequent solicitations addressed to Ms. Diether Haenicke. Fundraisers, take note!

We can't do much about family names. That's why first names are usually chosen with great care. Expecting parents often spend months to select just the right name for their progeny. Family tradition used to be a respected guideline. As our family is about to have a second grandchild baptized, I am mindful that Caroline Dorothea bears the names of her grandmother Carol, her great-grandfather's name Carl in its female form, and that of her German great-aunt Dorothea. My son and I carry on the names Kurt and Waldemar respectively in memory of two relatives who died as soldiers in WWI. But that tradition seems to fade. Young couples nowadays often choose names that just sound beautiful, lining up vowels and the right number of syllables to match the family name. I particularly like the sound sequence Sedona Dobson and also the cute little girl who goes by that name. However, some parents seem careless when assigning names. I am thinking of a friend in Chicago whose exceptional spirit and energy are not reflected in his name. His parents named him Robert Bobb, but everyone calls him Bob Bobb. My former assistant, Irene Stink, was in the habit of signing documents with her last name preceded by her first initial, which caused both consternation and smiles.

I am very comfortable with my name, difficult though it might be. But once, for about twenty seconds, I was in danger of losing it. When I became an American citizen thirty years ago, the presiding judge pointed out that my German name was not mainstream American and might not blend in properly. This was the moment to pick something more pronounceable, he helpfully advised. I asked for a suggestion. He made me sound out my name and then suggested "Peter Hennessy." I looked at my wife. She violently shook her head. And so I kept my identity. Peter Hennessy? Naah!

April 11, 2001

∾

Gentlemen regard restrooms as sanctuaries of privacy

In another column, I noted that a woman will sometimes publicly announce her departure to the ladies' lounge and that other women interpret this announcement as an invitation to join the excursion. Similar behavior in men would be met with amazement and even suspicion. I take this as another one of the many inexplicable idiosyncrasies that sets men and women apart.

Men have a different relationship to those islands of privacy and, unlike women, they don't consider them loci of gregariousness and social encounter. Men hardly ever enter restrooms for other than the obvious purposes, which they transact swiftly and with a minimum of talk. Acquaintances are greeted fleetingly, and eyes remain fixed firmly on areas above the shoulders. I always found useful my father's advice to wash my hands carefully afterwards, and to make absolutely sure that they are bone dry when leaving, so that any doubt and suspicion is removed from the mind of the first person who shakes your hand outside the restroom.

Several memories come to mind in connection with men's restrooms. Most restaurants display signs reminding their employees that they must wash their hands before leaving the bathroom. Once, in a fine restaurant in Paris, my cousin Willi stood next to the chef in the bathroom and noticed that he left straight for the kitchen without stopping first to wash up at the sink. This instilled in Willi such a lasting, generic suspicion about hygienic conditions in French restaurant kitchens that, whenever in France, he would eat exclusively boiled eggs and bananas—two foods he could peel himself—confident in the knowledge that his meal had not been compromised by potentially soiled human hands. He consumed the rest of his calories by concentrating on wine, giving no thought to the possibility that the grapes might have had contact with naked feet.

In Germany, many restaurants have personnel outside the restrooms who see to the facilities' cleanliness. One rewards them with a coin upon leaving. During my student days in Munich, we usually ate our early morning Weisswurst at the Donisl beer hall, when hoards of tired women would trot in from all over town and pay for their breakfasts with nothing but dimes. We started the day when the toilet women's nightshift was over.

Traveling with me in Germany, my friend Greg Dobson was once leaving such a guarded toilet but found himself without a coin. A big glass door separated the men's room from the restaurant, and I could see from the other side Greg trying to sneak by the toilet lady without paying her. However, to his horror, the glass door would not open, no matter how forcefully he pushed it. I saw the toilet lady shouting at him. Panic spread over Greg's face, because he could not explain to her his predicament in German. Had she locked the door by electronic device to stop freeloaders? After moments of agony and embarrassment, Greg was freed. Another customer, also leaving, opened the door with ease by pulling it. It opened only in one direction. The toilet lady had actually meant to be helpful. She had yelled to pull, not to push, which my friend had translated as: "Hey, fellow, you pay or you are stuck in here." Nevertheless, from then on Greg made sure he had a coin when the urge arose.

Another time, standing at a urinal at LaGuardia airport, I noticed right next to me a famous face: David Brinkley. I concentrated on my business. But another traveler approached him and asked the well-known and temporarily quite occupied newsman for an autograph. Brinkley exploded in anger. The rest of the crowd agreed that the principle of sanctuary had been violated and drove the autograph hunter away.

Forever memorable to me are the words spoken by my former boss, Wayne State University President George Gullen. We were engaged in our own very private business in a men's room on campus when a student entered, recognized the president, and cried out: "Good morning, Mr. President!" Mr. Gullen turned around and said calmly: "Call me George, young man. In here we are all peers."

November 8, 2000

≈

Will I see Fido in Heaven?

"If you want a friend in Washington, get a dog," Harry S. Truman, who should have known, allegedly mused to reporters. I remember Earl Bruce, the Ohio State football coach, expressing similar sentiments when no one but his pet mutt would greet him affectionately after a lost game.

It is this unconditional devotion that forges the powerful bond between us and our dogs, and only the most hardhearted brush aside the happiness that our pets' unconditional adoration provides. No matter what—they will stick with us. We can talk to them, and they won't talk back. They keep secrets better than any bosom buddy. They stand ready to defend us against any attacker. They are our true friends—Harry Truman was right.

We cat lovers have similar arguments to field. Our pets possess a grace and elegance that humans rarely display. Our cat may sit snuggled next to us through the length of a long evening read and, having been properly fed, will let us finish our book in peace—unlike the rest of our family.

We truly love our pets. We feel comfortable with them. We give them endearing names and are not embarrassed to shower them with more affection than we usually show our children and spouse in public. No wonder the PC movement has included our pets in its all encompassing re-naming campaign: pets have officially become our 'animal companions.'

I am currently between pet relationships and have to settle for the companionship of my family and their comparatively meager adoration. But this was not always so. I had my glory days, too, from the time our first cat, Patch, moved in with us. Although she was my children's pet, it was I who ventured out looking for her during a nasty blizzard; and I still think my family hoped more fervently for her rescue that it feared for my possible demise in the winter storm.

Patch eventually perished in Ohio, breaking through the ice of our swimming pool where I found her frozen the next morning. With tears in my eyes and an axe in my hand I freed her from the ice and pondered how I would bring the sad news of her death to my children. "I have bad news, children," I began at the break-fast table, and both immediately cried out: "Grandma died!" My mother had been ill, and both children loved her dearly. When I reported the demise of just the cat, their grief was tempered, luck-ily.

We buried Patch in the vegetable garden, and the following summer the raspberries growing on her grave were bigger and more abundant than ever before. The children did not notice the cause and effect of this circumstance, and my wife and I ate the raspberries with remorseful reluctance.

One cat later, we were adopted by Josephine. Although she normally preferred the outdoors after dark, she faithfully stayed at the foot of my sickbed through my three serious illnesses like a good nurse keeping watch through the long and lonely hours of the night. When Josephine turned eighteen and could no longer walk, no family member could bear the thought of bringing her to the vet and having her put to sleep. Her passing was mourned for a long time.

My only pets have been cats and dogs. Others harbor com-panionable emotions for horses or birds, even snakes and igua-nas. No matter how unusual the pets, their death is always mourned, sometimes in exaggerated ways. Pet cemeteries exist, some with clergy-assisted funerals, elaborate caskets, and expen-sive gravestones. Support groups like the 'Association for Pet Loss and Bereavement' have sprung up, and various web sites offer "genuine sensitivity and caring" and grief support chat rooms. Books offer spiritual guidance for the pet bereavement period, and the anxious question "Will I see Fido in Heaven?" is affirmatively answered by one Mary Buddemeyer in her book of the same title.

When an animal dies, so we are assured on *www.petloss.com*, it passes across the 'Rainbow Bridge' into Heaven where it is restored to health and vigor and awaits its owner for a "joyous reunion, never to be parted again."

Testimonials from pet owners with near-death experiences offer affirmation that the Rainbow Bridge truly exists. For those to whom this is not enough, an inspirational, and very bad, poem by Jan Cooper promises in its last stanza:

But an Angel just appeared to me,
And he said, "You should cry no more.
GOD also loves our canine friends,
He's installed a doggy door!"

That's a little much for me, as dearly as I loved my pets. I rather prefer the grave stone inscription I once found at the Presidio in California, where, right at the foot of the Golden Gate Bridge, the regimental mascots and pets of officers lie buried. Plain, but with a true sense of mourning and affection, it reads:
"Here lies Roscoe, the best damn dog we ever had."

That is an epitaph I would wish—with one slight modification—for myself.

March 24, 1999

∽

Techniques of appearing to be awake vary with age

I attend many board meetings, and I teach college classes. This enables me to offer some observations on generational differences in sleeping in public places.

I serve, mostly with people over fifty, on boards and commissions whose meetings start at 7:30 a.m. so that by 9 a.m. members can conduct their own affairs after having attended to those of the public. These meetings are unusually productive. The mind is rested and fresh, attention is focused and sharp, and things move and flow.

But other meetings take place late in the day when keeping focused becomes a challenge. One has to listen to presentations, which are often routine, and the challenge is to look attentive and not to doze off. This is particularly hard in meetings scheduled right after lunch or dinner, when a full stomach induces the natural desire to give one's eyes and brain a rest. This is particularly so if the lights are dimmed, and a speaker shows slides in the semi-dark.

I try to stay awake on such occasions by letting my eyes make the rounds, and I observe with envy and admiration my colleagues' finely honed skills of appearing to be awake. I know several who have mastered the art of sleeping with their eyes open. They even manage to stiffen their necks so that their heads stay straight without dropping occasionally on their chests. Only their deep and drowsy breathing gives them away.

Some have developed other artful ways of appearing awake. They freeze an attentive mien on their faces and give the impression that they close their eyes only to avoid all visual distraction, so that they may give the speaker their utmost attention. Others let their heads sink down on their chests, where their closed eyes cannot be seen, but have trained themselves to scratch their heads from time to time in a thoughtful gesture, indicating by this motion that they are actually awake and following the proceedings in pensive concentration. They are the true masters of deception.

Many people whom I observe in this state of half-sleep have undoubtedly learned their skills in college where the real virtuosos of open-eyed sleeping hold their perpetual convention. Here the effect of early and late meetings seems to be reversed. While I was president, I preferred to teach very early in the morning. However, 8 a.m. is an ungodly time for most undergraduates. The mind is not rested and fresh, attention is not sharp and focused, and things do not necessarily move and flow. I learned quickly that students are seldom fully functional before 10 a.m. A few of the students, having gone to bed around 3 or 4 a.m., interrupt their slumber briefly to get washed and dressed, then drag themselves to early morning classes where they sink peacefully and unabashedly back into Morpheus' arms.

They are helped by my reluctance to call on students who don't raise their hands, because I don't want to embarrass anyone who obviously does not know the answer. But what helps them even more is a recent development in youth culture. Ever since the baseball cap ceased to be a mere piece of clothing and became part of a youngster's anatomy, it can be worn in class. Professors would risk raised eyebrows were they to ask for the removal of this symbol of youthful self-expression. While outside the class the visor is mostly worn backwards or over one of the ears, in class the visor loses its self-expression and becomes a piece of protective clothing. Pulled down deeply over the face, it can hide the entire face down to the mouth, and unless the lower jaw drops and snoring sounds are emitted, nobody can tell if what rests below the cap is sleeping or not. The professor has to accept that his lectures seem to induce either enthusiasm or sleep, depending on the hour of the day.

I have learned my lesson. Now I attend board meetings in the early morning and teach classes in the late afternoon. I see much fewer cases of narcolepsy that way.

August 16, 2000

∽

Social thought and philosophy on the bumper sticker

I remember well a time when bumper stickers abounded. Practically each car in the university parking lot carried a message and often more than one. Most student cars sported slogans, maxims, and directional messages of one kind or other, advertising the cause du jour of its owner, coaxing every passer-by to save either the spotted owl, the whales, or, for those thinking globally, the whole Mother Earth.

Graduate students and some of the younger faculty, who had spent their student days protesting in front of administration buildings, preferred slogans that encouraged one to "Question Authority." Those bumper stickers usually disappeared as soon as the young profs found students in their own classes who did just that. Not surprisingly, the advice most fervently embraced on campuses was: "Make Love, Not War," a captivating message of universal enticement, particularly to the young.

Bumper stickers are so appealing to many people because they condense a strong sentiment or a political conviction into one brief line. Every philosopher and teacher longs to find a golden formula that encapsules a complex thought, or that makes an intricate concept understandable. We think of Descartes and remember one line: *Cogito ergo sum*—I think, therefore I am.

The bumper sticker and the T-shirt are pop culture's answer for those who wish to communicate to the world where they stand on the essential issues of the day. Unfortunately, this leads some people to believe that all thought can be expressed appropriately and sufficiently through maxims glued to car parts. These people I call the graduates of the Bumper Sticker School of Social Thought and Philosophy.

There are those innocent stickers that simply signal parental pride over the fact that "My Son is an Honor Student at Loy Norrix." But there is also the expression of distrust in public education which says: "I honor my student. I home school." Political stickers are the most boring, but even they can wander into borderline humorous territory. How about: "Don't steal. The Government hates Competition," or "Friends don't let Friends vote Republican," which plays on "Friends don't let Friends drive drunk." During the Clinton impeachment process, "Don't come back, Kid!" or "Jail to the Chief," had much popularity. Definitely ugly and deeply disturbing was one I found on a pickup truck in Northern Michigan which asked: "Lee Harvey Oswald, where are you now that we need you?" Even bumper stickers can play with the limits of the First Amendment.

Gun ownership, a deeply divisive political issue, has certainly entered the bumper sticker public arena. A frequently seen sticker is: "MY president is Charlton Heston." The further rural one goes, statements like these abound: "I Hunt to Live–I Live to Hunt," or "Ted Kennedy's Car has killed more People than my Gun," or the ever ready: "Guns don't kill People. People kill People." What a comfort to be able to reduce a very complex matter to one simple line! For contrast I like: "Support the Right to Arm Bears."

Practically all significant issues find their place on bumpers. A funny commentary on the sad state of health care cost is: "I became a Christian Scientist. It is the only Health Plan I can afford." The vegetarians want us to "Eat People, not Animals," which is advice I find hard to swallow. The anti-abortionists tell us that "The most dangerous place in America is in a woman's womb," whereas an opposing sticker advises: "If you can't feed them, don't breed them." Two horrifying simplicities. There are even stickers one might consider feminist. How about: "She who laughs lasts," or "I lost 180 pounds. My husband left me." Even religious issues are fully covered: "If you are living like there is no GOD, you'd better be right," or the hopeful: "When the last trumpet sounds, I'm outta here."

Driving behind Bumper Sticker School graduates, I seldom find myself intellectually enriched by their social commentary. Some of their sticker-sized thinking even frightens me. Only occasionally do I sympathize, as when I read: "Give me Chocolate and Nobody gets hurt." Now there's a thought!

July 26, 2000

～

Trials in a German hospital make it good to be home

One thing puzzles me. When I tell physician friends that I have to check into a hospital, they sometimes advise: "Be very careful!" What am I to make of that? Should I stay awake during surgery and make sure no instruments are left in my abdomen? Should I clean my own room to reduce the risk of infection?

I certainly had occasion to exercise some caution recently when I checked into a German hospital. Things there were startlingly different. Once admitted, I found myself in a room with two other patients, both women and very much my seniors. This situation revitalized my lifelong quest for privacy, particularly in medical settings. Three persons in any hospital room are two too many, especially if room occupancy is unisex. Even the usual American configuration of 'semi-private' rooms is uncomfortable for me. I believe there is no such thing as a semi-private room as much as there is no semi-pregnant woman. You either are, or you aren't.

Hospital gowns are the same in Germany as in the U.S.: back wide open. The unisex setting created distinct visual challenges since one of my roommates frequently walked by my bed to exercise her legs. The other woman, a recent refugee from Serbia, turned hostile when she realized that I was an American. One of

117

her relatives had been 'collaterally damaged' (the war in Yugoslavia being at its peak at the time), and she repeatedly shuffled over to berate the Great American Satan. My pleas to leave me alone in my struggle to recover from a heart attack went unheeded.

I considered this an environment not conducive to proper convalescence and focused my energy on obtaining a private room. I succeeded. After two days, during which my eyes and ears suffered severe collateral damage inflicted by my roommates, I was transferred to the only single room available: the one set aside for kidney transplant patients.

Patients in this particular hospital didn't wear wristbands or any other form of identification. Given my peculiar room assignment, this practice induced slight panic in me especially during the nights. My wife assured me, though, that survival with one kidney is possible should there be a case of mistaken identity.

Still, privacy was achieved, and my peace of mind returned on account of the unusual hospital food I was given. Although labeled "low fat," my tray always contained regular and strong coffee (to stimulate my heart?), cream for my coffee (10% fat), a generous portion of butter (82% fat) or margarine (40% fat) plus Camembert cheese (30% fat) with slices of very tasty bread. One of the doctors advised me that even beer was available to patients who could persuade their doctors that sudden removal of alcohol from their daily diet would have an unsettling effect. I passed on the beer.

Two days later, a single room in cardiology became available. Would I want it? I jumped at the chance to leave nephrology and triumphantly moved into a private room complete with WC/shower. Almost immediately a representative from admissions entered asking if I wanted to use the private bathroom. I replied: Not right now. But I had misunderstood. She meant: Did I want to acquire the right to use the private bathroom for an additional charge of 50 D-Marks per day? I inquired about other choices. The answer was: Down the hall. I agreed to pay but decided to ask my doctor for an additional diuretic to get my money's worth out of that unusual fee.

When scheduled for an ultrasound, I waited patiently in my

room for an orderly to put me in a wheelchair and transport me to the lab. When she showed up she told me to follow her on foot, because she already had another wheelchair patient and could handle only one. I did my best. But on one of the long corridors she outpaced me and entered an elevator that closed seconds before I reached it. A sign read: "Hospital personnel only. Access card needed." I wandered around on my own and finally found the lab. After the test was completed, the attendant told me: "Since you found your way down here on foot, I'm sure you'll have no trouble getting back to your room without help." Thus I experienced a new approach to physical therapy.

I must admit, though, that I received fine medical care over-all and made it back to Kalamazoo safely. However, when sick, one really prefers familiar settings. Being home again is a good feeling. Now, when I can't sleep at night, I don't count sheep. I count blessings.

August 4, 1999

∾

I 'develop relationships' with my books

Until recently I have valiantly refused to buy my books via the Internet. This resistance is undoubtedly caused by a personal idiosyncrasy that I find hard to shake.

Over a lifetime, I have developed a very peculiar relationship to books in general and to my own books in particular. Unlike my wife who, as a librarian, is always ready to 'weed' collections, I have a very hard time discarding any book I own. It is because, as bankers now say, I 'develop relationships' with my books.

If a book was given to me as a present, it becomes more than the book itself; it is also an extension of the friend who gave it to me. If I used a book as a student, it reminds me of the excitement I felt when I first read it. Others elicit memories of the circumstances under which they came into my possession: bought on that unforgettable trip, acquired in a Paris bookstore, mailed to me by the author, brought to me in the hospital to cheer me up. I am reminded of dark and happy hours alike in which my books were close companions, teachers, or entertainers who provided excitement, laughter, tears, aggravation, lessons, or consolation.

Since I find it so hard to separate myself from my books later, I choose them rather carefully. For this I need a bookstore where I can look at them carefully, weigh them in my hands, assess their paper quality, print type, and general esthetic appearance, read a few pages, put them back on the table, return to them a while later to make up my mind—it is almost like courting, something that is curiously both intellectual and physical.

Of course, the bookstore itself is important. It must be comfortable, well stocked and, ideally, there must be personnel with whom I can talk about my intended purchase, if I need to. For most of my life the latter was a given. One could ask for recommendations. What to bring to someone interested in the outdoors? In movies? In Africa? In early American settlements? People selling books used to know how to guide the buyer, since they tended to be readers themselves.

In many bookstores, typically smaller ones, this still is the case. But there are also stunning surprises. Some months ago, I promised my daughter to pick up a copy of *A Streetcar named Desire,* which we could not find in our house after a recent move that caused great disarrangement. Certain to find it in one of the new mall-sized mega-bookstores, I entered and searched the shelves. When I could not find a copy, I went to the counter where a young woman inquired kindly how she could help me. I replied that I was looking for a drama by Tennessee Williams.

Immediately she worked the keyboard of her computer. Having searched the screen, she looked up and said with stern conviction: "Sorry, there is no such author." I admitted that he was dead, but that I had read and seen many of his plays with my own eyes and offered to do the computer search myself. That she could not allow. But eager to assist the customer, she tactfully proposed: "Perhaps you have the name wrong. Could it be William Tennessee?"

What was I to say in the face of such disarming ignorance? Should I seek revenge by asking her if she had anything by the famous basketball player Longfellow? Or could she check if they had something by W. E. B. Du Bois in the original French, not in the English translation? Should I tell her that George Eliot was a woman, and that Steinbeck is not a piano?

Instead I smiled back, thanked her for her efforts and thought: "Diether, you are getting soft in your old age." Then I drove home, opened my computer and typed in: www.amazon.com. What a relief! They had heard of Tennessee Williams.

November 24, 1999

∼

Robin Hood is now a wealth redistribution consultant

Many little boys still dream of driving a fire engine, becoming a policeman, a knight, or even a robber like Robin Hood. While the latter two are not actually careers with a bright and realistic employment outlook, being a firefighter or a policeman remain on the catalog of solid possibilities. All four options obviously appeal to the excitement or adventure inherent in each of those vocations, and I guess little boys and girls seldom dream of becoming investment counselors or college presidents, for that matter. There is nothing in those jobs to set the imagination of pre-schoolers on fire—and right they are.

As the little boys and girls get older, their outlooks get more pragmatic, and the range of options expands enormously. I am often astounded to learn of a profession that even I have not heard about, but which already exists. In a recent ad I read that a delightful local actress is by profession the 'WKZO Morning Personality.' Is there also an 'Evening Personality' at the station, or one for the early afternoon? I suppose newscasters and announcers are now generically known as 'personalities,' meaning persons who regularly appear on radio or TV. Media-inflated lingo makes us forget what the word 'personality' once actually meant.

I see a major trend to give new, better sounding names to professions that have existed for generations. Thus, the salesman, saleswoman, or, more recently, the salesperson have all become sales associates, a denomination that not only addresses gender equity but also alludes to a warm, cuddly sense of belonging. Waiters and waitresses have become waitpersons or servers. "Hi, folks. My name is Brandon. I am your server tonight. Can I bring you guys something to drink before dinner?" is the new restaurant mantra. Some bartenders now call themselves mixologists (I have a calling card to prove it), and persons cutting one's hair are no longer barbers but hair stylists or beauticians. Sanitation engineers now take care of our garbage and sewage; in the garden we employ the lawn care professional; and since Rodney King all persons driving cars are called motorists.

All over the employment map, the 'specialists' are completing their triumphant march into the vocational registers. Letters are no longer typed by secretaries but by 'correspondence specialists.' A 'reading specialist' is not, as one might assume, a person who reads very well, but one who teaches children how to read. The old-fashioned personnel division has metamorphosed into the 'human resources department,' which is teeming with 'human resource specialists' and 'employee recruitment specialists.' The public relations division can't function without its 'news and communications specialists.'

In addition to these new feel-good names for age-old jobs, extremely lucrative and truly novel opportunities have arisen. Since people have forgotten how to conduct a civil and focused conversation, professional 'facilitators' are now needed for group discussions. The need to inform employees about race relations has spawned a highly paid army of 'diversity trainers' who teach captive audiences. People who can't, don't, or dare not speak for themselves, hire 'spokespersons' who inform the world what their speechless boss thinks or means to say. If the boss incautiously ever utters anything himself, the 'spin-doctor' quickly convinces the gullible public that the boss actually meant to say something entirely different. Millionaire 'spokesmodels' are nothing but well-known faces, with no opinion of their own, who are for hire to say anything a sponsor tells them.

On the sadder side of life, the professions of 'grief counselor' and 'bereavement counselor' have sprung up, together with the 'pre-need counselor' with whom you talk before any grief befalls you.

My own favorites are the 'dog walker,' now frequently found in larger cities where busy executives don't find time to bond with their pets outside the home, and the 'personal shoppers' who, I suspect, in many instances have better taste than the tired or overextended souls who hire them. As one who often hired and who believes in outside consultants, I was nevertheless surprised that consulting extends into every intimate corner of life. When my daughter was married, a local baker (a flour transformation specialist?) insisted that we work with his 'wedding cake consultant.' Now why didn't that job ever come to mind when I was a little boy?

October 18, 2000

≈

U.S. films export the image of dirty cop to the world

Any American traveling abroad is struck by the omnipresence of Hollywood movies. The last time I walked through the pedestrian area in downtown Munich, ten of the twelve movie houses were offering Hollywood fare. Bruce Willis, Tom Cruise, Julia Roberts, and Leonardo di Caprio are as much a presence in Europe and Asia as they are at home in the U.S.A. Movies made in America are among the hottest export commodities of our country.

But Hollywood exports not only its stars. Through films and TV shows it conveys to citizens of other countries vivid images of American life and culture. Sometimes those images are positive, albeit wrong. My mother, who was addicted to the TV series *Marcus Welby, M.D.*, concluded from what she saw on the screen that American doctors routinely make house calls, take half days off to console incurably ill patients in their homes, only send bills to wealthy people, and generally lead saintly existences. It was for her an article of faith that American physicians were far kinder, far more generous, and thus far superior to any others in the world. I never had the heart to tell her that this was just TV.

In Japan, on the other hand, we were frequently asked by concerned parents how safe it was for their children to attend American universities. Many thought that small towns like Kalamazoo were preferable to larger cities such as New York, Chicago, or Los Angeles, which, according to American movies and TV, were crawling with gangsters, bank robbers, drug dealers, and psychotic killers.

And, indeed, our entertainment industry creates these stereotypes. A predominant American leitmotif is that of the crooked cop. Hundreds of movies live on this theme, and it is not a new one. In many films depicting life on the frontier, the sheriff, the marshal, or the local judge are on the wrong side of the law—i. e. in the pocket of the rich landowner, in cahoots with the powerful builders of railroads, or otherwise on the take. Widows and orphans are brutalized by criminal lawmen; water rights are stolen by legal shenanigans, until the Lone Ranger rides in and sets things right.

This then finds its continuation in contemporary settings. We see police departments on the take. Policemen routinely commit criminal acts. Crooked cops rape, kidnap, steal drugs, or protect their trafficking; they murder innocents and gangsters alike, make evidence disappear, and for the proper bribe shield criminals from capture. Witnesses typically fear corruption and leaks in the police force, and are reluctant to cooperate with those appointed to protect them. To top it off, our movies add yet another stereotype. The occasional honest cop is harassed by half-witted lieutenants, captains, or the police commissioner, who do their level best to reprimand the effective cops and hinder them in their investigations. The Sylvester Stallone picture, *Copland,* stands representative for this situation, where an entire police department has gone bad and criminal.

In spite of all these upsetting scenarios, the good cop usually wins, against all odds, against the stupidity of his bosses, and against the pervasive corruption in his workplace. One is relieved to note this, because if it were not so, one would have cause to fall into deep depression. The foreigner who shapes his perceptions of America by seeing our movies and TV shows, must believe that our country is dangerous indeed, and that those representing the law must be viewed with suspicion.

Why does the entertainment industry paint this crassly negative picture of American law enforcement? Do Americans really have an attitude of caution and suspicion vis-à-vis police officers? Does our actual experience truly justify this depiction of American life? Or is all this done simply for greater dramatic effect, with the hero against everyone around him? I don't know the reason, but I am glad my mother used to watch *Marcus Welby* instead of *Miami Vice*. Otherwise she would have worried herself sick about her son in America.

October 17, 2001

~

Body odor: aura's aroma or olfactory assault?

Of all the many speeches I have given over the years, I very distinctly recall one in which the body odor of my audience was so powerful that I had to finish quickly for fear of fainting.

The situation was mainly the fault of Greg Dobson, at the time my trusted assistant. Always an enthusiastic supporter of the university's athletic teams, he had scheduled me to give a pep talk to the hockey team. What he had not warned me about was that I would speak in a windowless locker room, right after the players returned from the ice after a two-hour practice session. I used to swim competitively. When swimmers return to the locker room they do not sweat, and they do not smell. I grew up in farm country and have worked close to goats, but twenty men just off the ice in a small room blew the lid off all previous experiences. I love the hockey men, but far more overwhelming than their dedication were their odiferous evaporations.

I remembered this olfactory experience the other day while reading an interview with the English rocker Sting in the *London Sunday Times Magazine*. There the widely admired musician declared: "I don't like soaps, and I don't use anything like soap or deodorant... I actually like my own smell." How good for him!

Is it something British? My wife and I experienced difficulties years ago when attempting to purchase deodorant soap in London. What we found instead were strongly scented soaps which covered odors, but did not prevent or eliminate them. But Sting doesn't even go for scented soaps. He prefers none at all. However, chances that I'll ever sit next to him are minimal, and so I confidently leave his problem to those who admire him in spite of this unappetizing idiosyncrasy.

Odors are clearly a matter of habit and conditioning. My son does not faint in locker rooms, but when I took him as a little boy into a barn with pigs, cows, and goats he almost lost his meal. To me animals smell down-to-earth and wholesome.

Also, strong cultural differences exist. Dick DeVos once told me how much experimentation and research Amway puts into finding the right scents and colors for soaps, perfumes, and toiletries that go into Asian or Latin American markets. What may smell delightful to a North American nose, might be repulsive to a Korean or a Brazilian nostril.

Even garlic does not smell offensive in countries where it is a daily staple. I used to fortify myself for bus rides around Athens by eating as much garlic as the other passengers and after a week became oblivious to the smell. Only my mother's embraces became ever shorter and less cordial.

As a teenager, I often heard European travelers returning from the U.S.A. talk condescendingly about the 'American bathroom culture,' and I recall that American exchange students, who insisted on taking a shower every single day, were not only a nuisance and but an enigma to their German landladies. As children, we used to keep clean by washing with contortionist movements out of a washbowl and a ewer, both now elevated to the status of heirlooms and to be found only in antique stores. Since then, I have become addicted to the mocked American way of regular showering and have gratefully smelled on recent trips that Europe has finally Americanized itself in this area of personal hygiene.

Nevertheless, in many countries a distinct personal, shall we say, aroma is still perceived as quite stimulating and even sexually enticing. A European colleague of mine, a follower of New Age thinking, assures me that all too frequent bathing and soaping destroys the body's aura and thus its health. Last time I met him he was obviously in great health, because his strong aura greeted me the moment I entered the room.

Whether one welcomes body odors as erotic stimulants or conveyors of good health, all this is obviously a matter of degree and intensity, with hockey practice clearly producing too much of a good thing.

May 10, 2000

≈

Neighborhoods then and now

I live in a pleasant condominium development in Oshtemo. It is a contemporary neighborhood with a suburban feel, with nearly identical looking attached units—well-kept and attractively landscaped.

Most modern developments like ours are architecturally quite different from the neighborhoods I used to live in forty years ago. The houses on our street now are what some architects call snout houses, with wide driveways leading to two-car garages that protrude, like snouts, from the actual dwellings. A small walkway connects the driveway and the front door. The neighborhood is dominated by cars, and only walkers who are exercising pass by. In fact, there are no public sidewalks. Most people drive up to their condo, open their garage doors with a remote control, and enter their domicile directly from the garage. Neighbors wave at one another as they drive by, but they seldom meet in front of their houses. This typical suburban architecture does not facilitate meeting one's neighbors. That used to be quite different.

Shortly after I arrived as an immigrant in Detroit, I moved into a blue-collar neighborhood on the city's west side. It was a neighborhood that made being neighborly easy, even unavoidable. All the small houses, in which I and my neighbors lived, had ample front porches on which people would sit in the evenings and watch the world go by. From our front porches we would watch the neighborhood girls being picked up by their dates; we knew which neighborhood boys were up to no good; and *they* knew we were watching them. We knew who was on vacation or visiting relatives for a few days, and the entire neighborhood was watching the house in the traveler's absence. Neighbors would feel free to step up to one another's porches, often beer in hand, and sit down for a leisurely chat. It was called 'neighboring,' and sitting on the front porch was considered an open invitation to the neighbors to come by to shoot the breeze. On those evenings one learned who was ill, or who needed help in the form of meals, or babysitting, or transportation, and it was considered natural to offer and to accept neighborly assistance.

I was initially quite an oddity among my neighbors. Since I was seen reading books all day long, it was widely assumed that I was unemployed, and one or the other of my good neighbors would come over in the evening telling me of jobs that were open in their plants, and if I were interested, they would talk to the manager on my behalf. They were looking after my welfare in their own way, offering to be helpful, as good neighbors do. It was a sense of community that struck me as generous and giving, where we all knew one another, relied on each other, and where reciprocity was expected, but not demanded, and where favors were never counted.

With increasing affluence, our communities have changed. Many of us now own houses in more than one location, usually in other states, and we are absent from our home communities for many months at a time. Our houses tend to be farther apart from each other, and gated communities with uniformed guards and security cameras are doing much to separate people. When we build houses now, privacy is the key objective, and sidewalks and front porches that once made neighborhoods so inviting and inclusive have largely disappeared. We now build neighborhoods in which people can't go 'neighboring' any more by just strolling down the street.

The old city neighborhoods did have a different feeling of community and closeness. To this day, I remember those early neighbors: the children busily helping their families by taking paper routes or cutting their older neighbors' lawns. I remember the salesmen, the automobile factory workers, the waitresses and accountants, and the many young mothers helping each other raise their kids. I may remember that Detroit neighborhood with too much nostalgia, but it was a functioning and close community, and it was comforting and a pleasure to live there. I wonder if future generations will remember their suburban neighborhoods with similar nostalgia.

October 9, 2002

We need a monument for young mothers

I have a new job description. It includes singing, dancing, and other musical entertaining, reading, occasional chauffeuring, feeding meals, and lots of heavy lifting. I am, of course, speaking of my new role as grandfather, or 'Opa,' as I am referred to *en famille.*

I cannot yet claim perfection regarding my job performance. Reading and chauffeuring I do quite well thanks to skills acquired during previous employment. But singing and dancing, both new in my repertory of talents, not only test the limits of my artistic abilities but also my physical endurance. The greatest challenge, however, is the heavy lifting, which comes into play when grandchildren need to be picked up or must be carried around to be calmed and soothed. The latter, at times, may even require heavy lifting, singing and dancing all at once—quite a challenge for a man of my advanced age.

Most of these new skills come to me easily, and there probably has never been a job in my long career that has given me more instantaneous and lasting satisfaction. My two grandchildren— both girls, ages three years and eight months—live next door, and they visit, often several times a day. Obviously, my work generates a high degree of customer satisfaction, since they return regularly, smiling and happy, demanding more of the same services day after day.

Luckily, though, my new job is only part-time. It lasts only a few moments here and there, when I am supposed to hold and humor the baby while mother and grandmother are temporarily unavailable, or when I am drawn into a game of high imagination by the three-year-old. Then I have to pretend to be a bird, a fish, a car, or even the big bad wolf. At other times, the women command me to sit at the top of the stairs to prevent the crawling baby from falling down, or I have to chase behind the toddler to prevent her from harm that can come from sharp-edged furniture, flatware, heaters, cars, swimming pools, and the like. These are functions I can only fulfill part-time. More than twenty minutes of this, and I am near physical collapse—outrun, outjumped, outdanced, and outcrawled by my boundlessly energetic little granddaughters.

In such moments of sheer exhaustion, I often admire the wisdom of nature, which has placed childbearing and childrearing at that time of our lives when adult physical energy still matches that of babies and toddlers. And while I sink washed out into an armchair, I harbor thoughts of erecting a monument to all young mothers who energetically, gleefully, and with pride fulfill my part-time functions as full-timers. I see my own daughter handle this job of caring for two small children beautifully, and I see her many friends in similar situations. My admiration for these young mothers is genuine and measureless. Even if they have an occasional babysitter, these mothers devote practically all day to their children. Bathing, nursing, making meals, shielding the kids from harm, playing with them, ferrying them to playgrounds, pre-schools, libraries, pediatricians, shopping centers, and grocery stores—they face an endless array of activities that demand strategic planning, physical strength, saintly patience, and strict self-control.

Many of these full-time young mothers look upon lunch or dinner in a restaurant without a child in tow as a major treat. An undisturbed hour at home to write a letter or do some quiet reading they consider a rare gift. I know many such young women: I see them loading kids into cars, schlepping them through super-markets, organizing outings in parks with other mothers, and all the while they appear cheerful and competently in charge. They are my heroes. A monument to them, and a big one, is in order.

Then I look at my own wife, now a proud and doting grand-mother. I fear I did not appreciate enough, when I was younger, how terribly hard she worked when she raised our own two children. She once was one of those remarkable young mothers whom I now so admire. Her name belongs on that monument too.

July 4, 2001

∾

130

I want good service. Am I asking too much?

I have always found the American standard of customer service to be superior to that of Europe. Indeed, America has spoiled me in this regard, and I have come to expect good service wherever I dine or buy goods. Most cashiers, agents, waitpersons, and civil servants still provide that excellent service, and it seems many of them are enjoying their own good service as much as I am. I love going to the little post office in Oshtemo where the most helpful people in the entire U.S. postal service stand behind the counter. There are receptionists in our town whom their employers can't pay enough for the outstanding PR work they do for their offices. The courtesy of the staff at the D&W always draws me back to that store, and the friendly demeanor of the waiters at Hunan Gardens is just as enjoyable as the food they serve. These are just a few examples out of many.

However, there are also a few sorry exceptions, notably in checkout lanes at huge supermarkets. As I put my purchases on the conveyor belt, the cashier mumbles: "Hi, how are you today?" and before I have time to respond, she swings right back into an animated conversation with the cashier or the bagger next to her with whom she discusses the events of last night. Thus I learn that John didn't really mean what he said; he says that all the time, but he doesn't mean it, not really, he's just kinda kidding, like you know, sort of saying things, he's just that kind of a guy, you hear what I'm saying? All the while I stand there flabbergasted, left to my outdated notion that the customer should be paid attention. Whoever said that the customer was king? I feel like I am intruding on a kaffeeklatsch where private affairs are rehashed in seamless sentences.

Another type of service provider is the cashier or bagger who feels compelled to entertain the defenseless customer. As if he were on stage, he relates to his co-workers will full voice his take on the movie he saw: And man, did we laugh and laugh, it was just hilarious, everybody thought so, I can't tell you how funny it was, believe me, I was breaking up, that's how funny it was, what can I say?

Quite frankly, it is of little interest to me if John really meant what he said, and I can do without the complimentary and inex-pert movie review. All I want is the cashier's careful attention to my bill; I want no cracked eggs in the carton; and I don't want the bagger to bag the potatoes on top of the grapes. Is that asking too much?

Most customers are too tactful to interrupt such casual con-versations among store personnel. They accept as a fact of life that some young cashiers see customers only as insignificant flot-sam drifting by their youthful universe. But such inattention always irks me, and occasionally I speak up. As a result, rolled eyes meet my interruption, like hey man, we were talking, didn't you hear that? But if I put down $100 for two bags of groceries, I wish to have their prices properly recorded and the items most carefully packed.

What may be the reason that their service is so thoughtless? I often wonder if these mostly youthful offenders have ever seen really good, old-fashioned service themselves. Perhaps they don't know what it looks like. They have grown up in a world of self-service gas stations, self-service restaurants, and self-service stores. For them there may be no connection between service and customer. For them the entire world may be one of self-service. I have never accepted the term self-service, which I consider sim-ply a contradiction in terms: I don't see how one can provide cus-tomer service to oneself. They may see things differently.

But I still appreciate old-fashioned good service and take my business to wherever it is available. Thank heavens, it is still easy to find in most places in our community.

June 27, 2001

~

A German, a Pole, and a lawyer go into this bar...

I just finished reading a book of jokes about Germans, and it is one of the funniest collections I have ever seen. Most of the jokes, of course, build on the stereotypic perceptions people hold of Germans: their obsession with orderliness and punctuality, their well-known lack of humor, their assumed respect for authority, etc.

While laughing my way through the book, it occurred to me that I was violating a basic tenet. Whoever unleashes his humor these days along ethnic or racial lines unleashes simultaneously the wrath of the notoriously humor-free Politically Correct movement which advises us that ethnicity, race, and gender are exempted from all public jocularity. Only the fact that lawyers still are mostly white males accounts for so many lawyer jokes flowing freely from Rotary and Kiwanis rostra.

But ethnicity and its accompanying stereotypical images have been the basis of jokes for generations of comedians. There are perceptions of one or two 'typical' traits that characterize any given ethnic group.

Scotsmen are supposed to be excessively parsimonious. The Chinese are considered inscrutable. The English can't cook a decent meal and are sexually frigid to boot. The French, on the other hand, are supposed to be romantic and have developed love making to an art form. The Dutch are wholesome and scrub the sidewalks in front of their homes, when they are not busy making cheese. Russians are moody and given to melancholy songs. The list can be extended endlessly, particularly when one adds race, hair color (blonde only!), or gender.

The banishment of ethnic and racial jokes originates in the concern that jokes often expose an entire group to ridicule, belittling, and demeaning it. Further, it is argued, such jokes tend to perpetuate stereotypic prejudices to the detriment of the group members. This is a serious argument and not to be taken lightly.

However, one should perhaps differentiate between good and bad jokes, realizing that jokes are largely a matter of taste and judgment. Those which intentionally demean, belittle, and hurt people never belonged in the good jokes category anyway. But jokes can also poke fun at lovable and endearing idiosyncrasies of individuals and groups. Such jokes are warm and funny. And the problem with regulating humor is that no one likes being told what not to laugh about.

Many good jokes live on exaggerated and false stereotypes. One cannot tell a good lawyer joke without raising in the listener a particular anticipation of the joke's direction; and if a Polish joke is announced, one does not expect it to be about someone winning the Nobel prize.

While setting the stage and preparing us for the punch line, the stereotype never claims to expose a social reality. No person in his right mind truly believes a stereotype. I can name a Polish Nobel laureate; have eaten excellent meals in England; have encountered terribly messy people in Germany; have wondered about the wholesome Dutch while walking through Amsterdam; and know for a fact that lawyers are not the scoundrels jokes make of them. I claim no expertise, however, on the English being frigid or the French being the best lovers. Who other than an internationally promiscuous expert in comparative lovemaking could provide evidence about this stereotype?

Good ethnic and racial jokes have not disappeared. Comedians like Chris Rock and Eddie Murphy can and do tell jokes about African-Americans that would get a white comedian immediately castigated by Jesse Jackson or the PC thought patrol. Jewish comedians continue to tell jokes about their wives and mothers that no Gentile can touch. Some of the best blonde jokes are told by my strikingly blonde and very intelligent niece. As long as one is a member of the racial or ethnic group that the joke targets, it appears one can perpetuate ethnic or racial stereotypes safely.

Thus this category of jokes survives. And I'll continue laughing at what I choose. But I do play it safe: My ethnic jokes are all about Germans from now on.

P.S. The Polish Nobel laureate is Henryk Sienkiewicz, literature, 1905.

January 12, 2000

~

Achievement beats self-esteem in the real world

Kalamazoo Central High School occupies an expansive building on Drake Road. My son graduated from that school, and his parents were quite satisfied with the education he received there. In fact, he earned advanced placement credit in college based on the academic work done at Kalamazoo Central. We also liked the fact that the student body was racially diverse and from different social and economic backgrounds. Clearly a good public school with adept teachers, a good mix of talented students, solid academic curricula, and enjoyable athletic programs.

But to some that was not good enough. One day, giant letters appeared on its façade, declaring Kalamazoo Central a "WORLD CLASS HIGH SCHOOL." I think this self-imposed and meaningless classification was the brainchild of its then principal, an educator whose trademark was boundless exaggeration. When he left Kalamazoo for a job near Chicago, he promised his new community: "Our vision is to develop the greatest school district on the face of the earth." Quite a mouthful and clearly one up from merely world class. What comes next? The best in the universe? I would be perfectly happy with sending my children to the best school in the county or the state, but perhaps my ambitions are too low.

But here was even more hype. In the same interview, he also revealed his views on education as follows: "The formula for students' success is having vision, mission, passion, and leaving a legacy." The school board members in Hazel Crest found this an "inspiring and positive vision." I was less inspired by such verbiage. My own formula for students' success is still heavy on reading, writing, and arithmetic and fairly light on vision, mission, passion, and legacy.

I am choosing this example to point out several things that strike me as potentially harmful in education. First of all, some of us educators—thank heavens, not all!—are given to truly terrible bombast in our educational jargon. We claim unsubstantiated greatness and rank, or set simply ridiculous goals. We get intoxicated with hollow pretenses. We place image above substance. Good words such as vision, mission, and passion are splattered around carelessly and robbed of their true meaning. They become empty clichés. Education has, in such cases, been infected with the fatuous and deceitful hype of advertising, void of all modesty and realism.

Educators who employ such exaggerations have, I am sure, commendable intentions. They believe that this hype raises the self-esteem of pupils. It is supposed to make students feel good. In fact, we have studies that show American high school students ranking very low in their knowledge of math and science but leading students from all other industrialized nations in self-esteem. However, I think that hyperbole does not help our students. It cannot create a solid sense of self-value. I firmly believe that the only reliable self-esteem rests on having developed real skills, academic or other, and being able to use and test these skills in real life situations. That gives a student true confidence. No 'feel-good,' inspirational talk can replace real knowledge, true learning, and hard work.

I further fear that unreflected use of the 'world class' label cheapens a high standard. The constant bombardment with hype may eventually lead youngsters to believe their work really is world class when it usually is not, and deep disappointment follows when their false self-esteem is exposed in college. I have seen too many freshmen who want to be engineers do math on the ninth-grade level. While self-esteem is highly desirable, a solid knowledge of math and physics usually gets the aspiring engineer better results.

A few weeks ago, the boastful inscription at the school was removed. The superintendent tells me that in the future its real name, Kalamazoo Central High School, will be displayed. The teachers at the school should be pleased with that. Let them continue to run, as they always did, a very good public school whose students get their self-esteem from solid academic accomplishments and not bombastic rhetoric.

September 12, 2001

~

Indoctrination is a crime against children

When terrorists struck America, my wife and I watched TV around the clock in shock, horror, and disbelief. My wife still follows the news almost hourly, interested in each new story and listening to expert analysis, debate, and commentary. I had to wean myself off the screen. Although I am a news junkie, the incessant occupation with the war on terrorism and the anthrax threat was beginning to take its psychological toll on me.

In such situations I tend to practice my own form of academic escapism. I retreat from the contemporary world by submerging myself into another, distant period of history. This, however, does not always work. The other night I had retreated to the Middle Ages, poring over old maps detailing the fortifications of Orléans while the English laid siege to the city in 1429. I thought I was safe in the 15th century, but suddenly my wife beckoned me to the TV room to see a startling newscast. Reluctantly I trotted back into the 21st century.

I saw a nice but somber looking Pakistani child of about six years being interviewed by an American reporter. The little boy was a pupil in one of the numerous schools maintained by the Taliban that offer meals and shelter to poor and often orphaned children, together with instruction in the teachings of the Koran. The child had been totally brainwashed and produced a litany of hateful statements that he obviously did not understand. He pronounced his scorn and abhorrence for America, his utter hatred of all things American, and his determination to commit his life to fighting the foreign devils. Had he ever met an American? he was asked. No. The reporter was the first American he had ever seen. Did he know where America was? Again the answer was no. What did he want to be when he grew up? He would of course join the Holy Jihad and destroy America.

The little boy with the angelic looks gave this recitation without a smile but also without great passion, almost casually, as children sometimes repeat rote learning. His teacher, present throughout the interview, smiled, however, gleefully satisfied with the results of his successful indoctrination.

I was deeply affected. Just a few weeks earlier, I had come across a class photo taken in my elementary school in Germany in 1941. My first grade teacher smiles benevolently at her forty little charges, all of them with soft, beautiful children's faces. I took a long look at myself, a nice, pleasant looking little boy sitting in the front row right under the big photograph of a stern, watchful Adolf Hitler on the wall above me. The classmate behind me, slightly mentally retarded, later unexpectedly died of pneumonia. Actually, he had been murdered through the euthanasia program for the 'eradication of unworthy life.' What a class photo!

The Taliban boy and I at his age do not have too much in common. After all, I was taught to read and write and do mathematics and was taught science, the arts, and music. But the innocence we had as children was similarly and criminally abused. Like he, I was taught to despise certain people because of the way they looked, dressed, or worshipped. Like he, teachers indoctrinated me with hateful and dangerous perceptions of people who were outside the locally declared norms. Like he, I was taught and encouraged to grow up to destroy people, ideas, and values that I did not even understand.

Hearing the little Taliban boy talk made me immensely sad. I realized that all over the world and throughout the ages trusting and impressionable children have been and are still being indoctrinated with hate, bitterness, violence, falsehoods, and lies by teachers, parents, religious leaders, and politicians. I will never understand nor will I forgive those who destroy our children's innocence with teachings of hatred and prejudice. I hope that the little Taliban boy will have my lucky fate: that he is saved from hate and violence, as I was, before it is too late and the terrible message grows into conviction.

October 31, 2001

~

Do we need better prepared teachers?

Both my children attended public schools in three different communities, were happy there, were well-prepared for college, and were taught by caring and competent teachers. My wife and I feel respect and gratitude for the women and men into whose care we entrusted our children for thirteen years. So what does the grim news mean that we recently find in the papers? Can it be true?

In Hawaii, 50% of newly hired teachers could either not complete or failed to pass their state certification exam.

In Long Island, N.Y. a superintendent gave applicants for teaching positions an eleventh-grade English test and found that only 25% could master it.

In Massachusetts, 59% of 1,800 would-be teachers failed the basic tenth-grade test in language, math, and other subjects.

President Clinton, in a budget message, challenged the states to conduct exams for prospective teachers evaluating their knowledge of the subjects they plan to teach. "In too many schools," he said, "teachers don't have to have college majors—or even minors—in the subjects they teach."

A 1996 report by the National Commission on Teaching and America's Future concluded that 25% of the nation's public school teachers were not fully qualified to teach in their subject area, this number being even higher in poor rural and urban school districts. In schools with the highest minority enrollment, only 50% of the children have a chance to have a math or science teacher with a degree in these fields. This confirms my suspicion that those who need it most, still get the worst deal in education.

Another study presented at the recent annual meeting of the American Association of Colleges for Teacher Education warned against raising the passing standards on tests for teachers. Raising standards would lead to having teachers with greater academic ability, but it would dramatically decrease the ethnic diversity of the teacher population. What a choice!

I see three reasons for this dilemma.

First: Many education colleges have allowed their curricula to shift too much from academic content to educational methods. The problem of insufficient academic preparation of teachers will not be solved until the proper balance between content and method is re-established.

Second: For most of this century, our schools relied on the many talented and bright women who sought professional careers, but whose typical few options were teaching, nursing, and librarianship. Ever since other, more lucrative, professional schools began to actively recruit women this trend has changed.

Third: We have known for twenty years that students majoring in education have, as a group, lower SAT scores than students in other subjects. Education colleges cannot be as selective in their admissions as law and medicine. Just imagine for a moment what a highly qualified national teacher corps we would have if the financial rewards of becoming a teacher were comparable to those of becoming a physician. Our schools of education could have the selectivity of medical colleges, resulting in similar standards of care in education and medicine.

It is a blessing that many talented young women and men still choose teaching as their profession. Given the complexity of our schools' social problems and their often disrespectful students, whose litigious and anti-authoritarian parents are of no help, teaching in today's schools is harder than most of us imagine. The frequent lack of academic preparation of teachers certainly needs to be addressed, but in the larger scheme of things it may be the smaller problem.

I give President Clinton's initiative due credit, but am not optimistic in my outlook. I fear the proposals for national teacher testing are dead on arrival. Massive and fundamental changes in our entire social structure are necessary before our schools can truly be healed.

June 9, 1999

~

Should English be spoken in our high schools and post offices?

The *Detroit Free Press* recently reported a fascinating fact. During the graduation ceremony at Western High School in Detroit, the valedictorian delivered her speech in fluent Spanish. A brilliant student of foreign languages? No, a Mexican immigrant graduating from a Midwestern high school with a large Latino population. While the non-Hispanic students wondered why their valedictorian was giving her address in Spanish, so the *Free Press* reports, the Latino parents cheered the speaker on. Owing to increased numbers of Mexican immigrants, the school is now 60% Hispanic. The principal, soon to be removed from the school, sat by expressionless. Latino community activists had demanded and been promised a Hispanic principal. The pressure is on for more teachers who speak Spanish. The administration, so Latino parents contend, is 'insensitive' by hiring teachers who speak only English in an American high school. Obviously, progress is now being made on the linguistic sensitivity front. But I should add that the Hispanic dropout rate at Western High has soared to 77%, 20% higher than the district as a whole.

Another anecdote, from Miami. While on vacation in Florida, I visited a post office where most customers appeared to be Hispanics. The very friendly postal clerk took ample time to help those with poor knowledge of English and to make sure they were served properly. But the woman in front of me flat out challenged the clerk and bombarded him with a fast barrage of Spanish. When he asked her to speak slowly, it turned out that she could speak English, for she berated the poor man in foul and fluent English for his insensitivity at not speaking Spanish. "Madam," he finally exclaimed, "you are in the United States. This is a United States post office. I have every right to speak English."

Obviously, immigration is not what it used to be. Previous generations came to this country to become Americans as quickly as possible. They realized that in order to succeed in business, education, and politics they had to learn English fast and well, and, unfortunately, they sometimes even forbade their children to speak anything but English. Having escaped often stifling traditions and choking economic circumstances, they were eager to learn, understand, and adopt the new country's political, economic, and social traditions—all with the intent to advance and to succeed in America.

But the face of immigration is changing. Ever-increasing numbers of new immigrants desire to have their own languages spoken at work, in public offices, and in our schools. An executive order (EO 13166), signed by President Clinton in the waning days of his presidency, requires every government agency and government contractor to provide all official paperwork, forms, and services in any language requested. Aside from the unimaginable burden on contractors and agencies ("May I please take my driver's test in Urdu?"), this order essentially makes the U.S. a multilingual country. Legislators on every level are afraid to declare English the official language of our country, because they fear to lose the ethnic vote.

Having taught in departments of foreign languages most of my life, I deeply believe in and have seen the value of being bilingual or even polyglot. I love the cultural richness foreign cultures and languages bring to our own national culture. I love to see cultural and ethnic heritages preserved in families and communities. I am delighted when parents speak French, Spanish, Mandarin, or Arabic with their children. But given the enormous variety of ethnic backgrounds in our country, we need English as our one common and official language so that we can all fully participate in our public, civic discourse. To succeed in education, the most powerful tool for social advancement, is to have an excellent command of English. My English was poor when I immigrated, but I did not claim that texts and tests were biased against me. Instead, I bought myself a dictionary. It taught me how to give a good commencement speech in English and also how to buy stamps at the U.S. post office. With a dropout rate of 77% and poor English skills any kid is doomed. Let's not allow that.

September 5, 2001

∼

Does politically correct speech really help?

I recently remarked that "anyone who believes that the Holocaust never took place, needs to have his head examined." This triggered a violent reaction in a feminist interlocutor who called my statement offensive. However, her sensibilities were not aroused by my insistence that the Holocaust had undoubtedly taken place; her indignation focused on my linguistic inadequacy. I ought to have said "should have *his* or *her* or *their* head examined," she sternly enlightened me. I was dealing, of course, with a person incurably inflicted with the zeal for politically correct speech.

From that point on, our conversation drifted away from substance and importance to the essentially humorless orthodoxy of PC speech patterns, which have loaded our communications with linguistic atrocities. Anyone, who sees more significance in a discussion of 'his and her' than in a debate of the 'No Holocaust' theory, I say it again, needs to have her head examined.

PC sensibilities reach into every corner of our lives. On PBS, a commentator remarked that someone at age 39 was too old to play professional football. A caller, 39 years of age, felt offended by the term 'old' and wanted it replaced by another term. This one incident reveals the broad PC tendency to rename things. By giving it another name, it is obviously assumed, fact or substance can be changed. My aunt was deaf; now she is hearing impaired. Others call her differently abled. Yet others see her as physically challenged. Does that name change improve her condition? Her self-esteem? Does she now feel better about being deaf? No. The word 'deaf' is a good word. It is descriptive and unambiguous, and I can't imagine that in anyone's mind it was ever meant to be demeaning or derogative. Would I, who am bald, feel better by calling myself follicly challenged? The almost allergic PC reaction to words like deaf, blind, old, bald, short (three of which accurately describe me) reminds me of Victorian prudishness which turned underpants into 'unmentionables' and expected women to faint when words such as brassiere or condom were spoken.

Renaming is also big in ethnic and racial contexts. Since my arrival in the U.S. in the early sixties, the PC name for one racial group has changed several times from Negro, black, colored, of color, Black, Afro-American, and now to African-American. We now refer to Native Americans rather than to American Indians, a name that many Native Americans, who speak of Indian Nations and Indian reservations, prefer. There is still debate whether the names chosen by sports teams were selected as derogatory references to American Indians or out of admiration and pride.

Many PC proponents are ardent feminists, many of them quite aggressive and offensive in advancing their own linguistic agenda. Who doesn't remember the stereotype of the 'male chauvinist pig'? A few years ago, a woman legislator wrote a book entitled *The only Boobs in the House are Men.* I can't imagine a male lawmaker getting away unscathed with a similar title on a book about female legislators.

I will concede that the PC movement has raised some valid points, but on the whole it suffers from being orthodox, schoolmasterly, self-righteous, and certainly without any liberating humor. At the time when light bulb jokes were rampant, I always found this one very good and typical. Question: How many feminists does it take to change a light bulb? Answer: That is not funny.

May 30, 2001

∾

IV. Memories:

Of Times and Places Past

Memories of the Holocaust

In the night from the 8th to the 9th of November 1938, all over Germany Nazi hooligans desecrated synagogues and set them on fire, demolished the businesses of Jewish merchants and bankers, and committed unspeakable cruelties against their Jewish fellow-citizens. Over ninety Jews were slain that night, thousands severely beaten and twenty to thirty thousand arrested or taken into 'protective custody' by the Nazi authorities. By and large, the general citizenry stood silently by and watched, looked fearfully the other way, or just let it happen.

The 'Night of Broken Glass' when Jewish shop windows were shattered was not, as the Nazis proclaimed, a "spontaneous outburst of anger against the Jewish parasites." It was a staged rehearsal, a test to see how the general population would react to a systematic government attack on an unprotected racial and religious minority.

Sixty years later, I happened to pass through my little home-town of nine thousand on the anniversary of that night. A silent memorial march was planned by the Christian churches in town, and a slide presentation on the area's vanished synagogues was to be presented by a local historian. Of the more than two hundred Jewish families estimated to have lived in town in 1938, none are left.

As I was sitting with some of my old school chums in the local pub that night, we could not tear ourselves away from this topic. All national historic events also take place on the very personal local level. They mark the lives of ordinary people; and, as the case may be, they burden or elate the participants or bystanders forever.

We were all children, three or four years old, when our local synagogue went up in flames. But our parents, our teachers, the local authorities, to whom we looked up during our youth, must all have been eyewitnesses or possibly even active participants, we realized. As we talked about those years which ended when we were ten or eleven years old, clouded memories began to surface. We remembered that one of the streets in town had been called "Judengasse," obviously because many Jewish families had their homes there. Today it is named after Carl Schurz, the German-American anti-slavery journalist and politician of Lincoln's times. We remembered some of the Jewish stores that, for a while, kept their original names after their owners had been expropriated and deported. I remarked that, inquiring at the local bookstore, I had not found any literature on the former Jewish presence in town, although I did stumble on an image of the vanished synagogue in a collection of historic photographs from the city archives. The old Jewish cemetery still exists at the edge of town, the tombstones overgrown, the gates chained. Few visitors ever find their way to it.

Just as our teachers remained silent after the war, the older people in town do not speak about that part of their personal history. When I inquired at the local newspaper about the memorial march, I was assured that it would be poorly attended. About sixty people marched that night.

One of us at the table knew and mentioned the names of the three ringleaders of the raid on the synagogue. All names were familiar to me. One of the men regularly cut my hair when I was a schoolboy, another was a minor city official when I grew up. Only one of them is still alive, in his eighties, a feeble and toothless old man. The only local records of that night are to be found in the police archives. Several non-Jewish citizens reported what they witnessed to the local police, asking that charges be brought against the perpetrators. This was an act of great courage at the time. The police did not act on the reports.

It was a somber evening for me and my friends. A small town had been touched by the great evil that the Nazis brought over their country. Over time, the town's citizens, for shame or out of convenience, had silenced their memories of the dreadful past. The two hundred families who once lived among them are now forgotten.

And we, the generation of children, have no real memories, but shudder at the thought that we could have been born a generation earlier. Would we have been silent, like many of our elders?

"Sad the country that has no heroes; and sad the country that needs heroes," writes Bertolt Brecht, who went into exile during Hitler's reign.

January 20, 1999

⁓

Iraq, seen through the dark lens of Germany

When I was a boy, my parents occasionally spoke French at the dinner table. They did that whenever a subject arose that they considered not fit for our ears, and one of my father's stock phrases was: "Helene, prenez garde devant les oreilles des enfants!" Which simply means: "Watch out, the children are listening." It is, to this day, a standard quotation among my siblings and me.

In later years we realized that my father often spoke these warning words when my outspoken mother veered into dangerous political topics. She might have remarked that for weeks no flour could be had at the grocery store, or that a neighbor's family had already lost their third son in the war, or that the mail from a recently bombed city, where relatives lived, was not coming through, and that she was worried. Such utterances, if repeated by a child to a party-line teacher, might have been considered defeatist and 'apt to destroy the heroic will of the German people to fight the barbaric enemy to the last drop of our blood.'

I know that all historical comparisons are usually inappropriate or at least highly problematic. But nevertheless, these days, when I see reports from Iraq, I am often reminded of the dark days of my youth.

Pictures of the great leader were omnipresent. They hung in every classroom, in every public office, in every waiting room, and bus station. While Saddam is usually seen firing 'celebratory shots' from a rifle, Hitler was shown, also mostly in uniform, with steely eyes gazing into our thousand-year future. The cult of personality is one of the strongest columns of an effective dictatorship.

As in Iraq, there was no freely elected parliament in the Germany of my youth. All means of communication were controlled by the state. The Goebbels Ministry of Propaganda tightly regulated radio, newspapers, and publishing houses. Our teachers never spoke freely on any subject but instead carefully toed the party line and taught us songs, poems, and stories of people who had died heroically for the fatherland. Telling jokes about political leaders meant inviting a death sentence.

The Nazis practiced 'Sippenhaft,' which meant that the entire family was punished for the crimes of one of its members. Saddam knows that principle, and his people know that he is likely to kill not only any scientist who speaks openly to the weapons inspectors, but perhaps his entire family. Sippenhaft really works.

Jews, homosexuals, and political enemies were brutally suppressed or murdered in German concentration camps. Saddam spreads poisonous gas on whole villages when he meets opposition from his own people. Prior to the war, inspection teams from Geneva, Switzerland occasionally visited the German death camps and interviewed the inmates who, of course, dared not tell them anything that was really going on. The foreign visitors found chamber music groups and literary circles in the camps, noted hard but not intolerable conditions, and were told that most of the inmates were actually 'in protective custody' to shield them from the wrath of their fellow citizens. Nobody, except a maniacally suicidal person, ever talks to foreign inspectors inside a brutal dictatorship that believes in Sippenhaft justice.

Later, while I sat through terrible bombing raids with little to eat and to wear, the Nazi functionaries hid in their well-guarded, luxurious country estates. Fieldmarshall Goering became the living example of obesity while the general population lived on meager rations. I think of Hussein's numerous presidential palaces and his well-laid table when I see the citizens of Baghdad fighting to survive.

When in 1938 the British Prime Minister Chamberlain returned from his meeting with Hitler in Munich, he triumphantly declared having found "peace in our time." Driven by their blind desire to avoid war, the Western powers had been fooled by a shrewd dictator who had evil on his mind all along. There was no absolute certainty, no smoking gun about Hitler's atrocious intentions. The inspectors did not find enough proof; and the Western political leaders wanted peace, peace at any price.

For this, the Allies later paid a horrible price in blood, sweat, and tears. At least one little boy would have been very happy if there had been a 'regime change' while there was still time. And he still believes that dictators are ruthless, untrustworthy, and truly evil.

February 5, 2003

~

Even hard times can produce golden memories

My friend Christian came last month for a brief visit. He was on his way to Florida where he maintains a second home, which he visits several times a year when he and his wife seek leisure and sunshine. I have known him for almost sixty years, since the war relocation program brought us to the same small German town and placed us together in second grade. Christian stayed all his life in the same rural town, married a local girl in the church in which we were both confirmed, studied English and religion, and eventually became headmaster of the school we once attended. Although my own life took an entirely different direction, our boyhood friendship stayed with us despite two very different lives on two very different continents.

We are now two elderly and reasonably well-to-do grandfathers, but whether we walk the beaches in Florida or sit in a sidewalk café in Europe, we love to look back at our early years as young boys, and we remember those years as happy, rich, and wonderful. How can it be, we sometimes ask ourselves, that we have these golden memories, when in fact we grew up amidst bombing raids, our fathers gone to war, with shabby clothes on our backs, and hardly anything to eat.

Our boyhood poverty would strike any of our children or grandchildren as extreme. Since shoe leather was needed for the war effort, we wore wooden sandals or clogs to school. I now see them sold as cute curiosities in gift shops. For me they were once a real piece of clothing. We both had to help gather food for our families. With our little hoes and buckets we followed the farmers at harvest, and whatever sliced and cut up potatoes, turnips, or heads of grain were left in the dirt by the big harvesting machines were ours to take home to scrub and to eat. On the way home, we would often satisfy our thirst right from the cows in the fields before the farmers came to milk them. When I once demonstrated to my kids, children of the big city, how to direct a stream of milk from the cow's udder directly into my mouth, they were impressed—but disgusted.

Christian and I, in return for a bowl of hot soup and five pounds of potatoes, would rent ourselves out for a whole day, and, bent on our knees, would help the farmers pick potato beetles off the new crop. In the fall, when strong winds had stormed through the area, our mothers would send us out before daybreak to gather apples, beech nuts, or tree branches that had been shaken down during the night in the community-owned orchards and forests. What had fallen to the ground could be taken; picking from the tree was theft.

At our church confirmation, Christian and I wore our first tailored outfits made from discarded suits once owned by our fathers. The cloth had been turned inside out and then stitched together again by well-meaning but inexpert mothers. My confirmation presents were three white linen handkerchiefs from my mother and a pair of cufflinks from my father. Many years later, long after my father had died, I bought myself a shirt with French cuffs and wore the cufflinks for the first time.

Why are our memories golden? I guess as young boys we never realized we were poor, because everyone around us was poor, too. We had all the important things children need. We had very loving parents who protected and guided us well. We learned to live with little and to be happy with it. We were taught how to work and how to shoulder responsibility, and it did not seem to burden us. We had friends who stuck with us. We learned that it feels good to help each other. We also never forgot how it feels to be hungry.

Today, Christian and I still like to sit next to each other, as we did in hard times a lifetime ago, grateful for our wonderful boyhood years whose rich memories nourish our friendship.

May 23, 2001

≈

German reunification inspires joy, appreciation of freedom

This month, Germany celebrates the tenth anniversary of its reunification. Most of us remember vividly the events of 1990: the fall of the wall that divided the city of Berlin; young and old dancing joyfully in the streets; emotional reunions among old friends and family members; tears, laughter, festive concerts, jubilant marches, pubs filled with people singing, drinking, and hugging each other.

Shortly before the end of communist rule, I had indicated in a European newspaper interview that I did not expect to see German reunification in my lifetime. I was not alone in that opinion. Even President George Bush, with presumably the best intelligence service at his disposal, revealed later that he was taken by surprise when the news of the collapse of the East German communist regime reached him.

The reunification of Germany ranks among the most emotional moments in my life. This had to do with my intense personal memories. I was a boy of ten when the separation took place. During the last months of World War II, my parents realized that the war would be lost (but did not dare discuss that knowledge in front of their children), and that we would soon be occupied by foreign troops. The Nazi propaganda machine in the schools painted a gruesome picture of the atrocities that would be committed by the invading armies. Like all children, I believed what the party officials told us, and I was frightened to death about what was to come.

When the German troops retreated, we hid for days in the dense woods surrounding our little town and watched the foreign soldiers advance along the country road towards our homes. They were all black. We recognized them as Americans, and were jubilant. Not knowing which lines had been drawn in Yalta by Stalin, Roosevelt, and Churchill for the division of Germany, we considered ourselves lucky to be occupied by Americans—and not the Russians. The Americans advanced about three miles beyond our house and settled in. We were safe. The Werra, a little stream the size of the Kalamazoo River, in which we children swam in summer, became the border on the other side of which the Russian troops took positions.

The years passed. As relations among the Western allies and Stalin soured, the Iron Curtain descended, and the border became impenetrable. Over the years, on my way to school, I saw from the school bus the gradual fortification of the border. Right through the beautiful farmland behind the river the communists strung a barbed wire fence, erected watchtowers with machine guns on top, cleared a wide band of land to give the guards good sight to shoot, and sowed landmines along the border. I remember seeing the border guards with their German Shepherds patrolling the fence, and at night I occasionally awoke when roaming deer triggered one of the landmines. We no longer swam in the river.

On our way home from school we sometimes stopped at the roadside when we saw farmers, under heavy guard, work the fields beyond the water. We would wave or shout a greeting, but they seldom waved back. I always wondered what they thought of us. We lived by then in a world of plenty, could travel all over the world, held real elections, spoke our minds freely and without fear, could read any book we wanted; and all that separated us from our less fortunate countrymen was a small river that might as well have been as broad as an ocean. Beyond that, it had been just good luck that three world leaders in Yalta had drawn a line on a map that put us on the better side of fate.

Those glances across the Werra River were my daily lessons in appreciation of democracy, liberty, freedom of speech, and plain good fortune. Needless to say, as a result of these lessons, I cannot understand how people who have the right to vote freely and to express themselves at the ballot box, stay home on election day. They should have stood next to me just once looking across that river.

I am not a citizen anymore of the country in which I was born long ago. But as it celebrates this important anniversary, my heart rejoices.

October 25, 2000

∾

151

Giving thanks to teachers who gave so much

Thanksgiving makes us think of our many blessings, and we feel a need to express our appreciation for all those who bring love, warmth, and meaning to our lives. While there are many such people, I would like, this year, to say thanks to teachers. Many of them have a profound influence on our children and grandchildren, and most of us remember some of our own teachers vividly for the rest of our lives.

This first occurred to me at alumni meetings throughout the country when men and women, who were graduated thirty or forty years ago, asked me if some of their old professors were still teaching. And as they mentioned their names, fond memories brought smiles to their faces. The alumni would remember specific classes, pithy remarks their teachers used to dispense, idiosyncrasies and eccentricities came to the fore, and as they spoke of their old teachers, friendly laughter warmed the remembrances.

My own memories of a special teacher go all the way back to first grade. As most children, I was very timid when my mother dropped me off at the school door; but I also remember the great excitement I felt about entering this new world of elementary school. Inside I was met by Frau Heppe, my first teacher, whom I will forever remember because she taught me how to read. She must have been in her forties, but I remember her as very old. The rumor in school was, and this was carefully spread by the older pupils, that instead of sending you to the principal, she would direct unruly students to her husband, the local dentist, about whom fanciful stories of unbearable torture abounded. My older siblings, who had undoubtedly fallen victim to the same myth when they entered school, further embellished such stories rather than ease their little brother's considerable anxieties.

The rumors made me pay careful attention to Frau Heppe's instructions, and in record time she taught me how to read. I keenly remember walking down the main street of our little town one day, and suddenly the mysterious ciphers on houses and storefronts began to change. They turned into letters whose meaning Frau Heppe had taught me, and then the letters turned into words that I could make out. I read "grocery," "bakery," and "bookstore," and I remember being overwhelmed by this new power transferred upon me by my first teacher.

Frau Heppe never did me any harm. She must have appreciated the eager student, and I loved her because she was a warm, caring, and patient teacher. But the encounter with her husband-dentist came nevertheless; only it was not Frau Heppe but my own trusted mother who one day took her trembling son to his office—another experience that turned out considerably less gruesome than my siblings and school folklore had led me to fear.

Perhaps these two early experiences with the teacher-dentist couple taught me the value of questioning what others say; the value of finding out for oneself; of not relying on rumor, vagueness, and hearsay, but to find truths, to ask and to question, and to build one's knowledge on facts and experience. In short: I relied on learning. I did not know at that time that my love for learning would grow ever stronger the more I advanced in school. Eventually it grew so powerful that I decided to stay in school for the rest of my life.

After Frau Heppe, more good teachers stood at my side and guided me. As I attended school after school and later several universities, many new worlds opened up before me, and at each entrance stood a teacher. So many of them gave me so much, taught me, helped me along, and mentored me. They have become part of me, and I am immensely grateful to them.

And as I remember my own mentors, I give thanks to all teachers for their dedication, their patience, and their care, and for the hard work they are doing. And I am grateful for the many liberties we enjoy in our country, among which the absolute freedom to teach and to learn without limitation ranks high.

November 21, 2001

153

A black market journey for Beethoven

A teenager today with $15 for a CD and any interest in good music at all can easily listen to the world's best orchestras and soloists. When I was that age and falling in love with Schubert and Brahms, all I had were two musicians and a piano tuner who opened for me the doors to classical music.

Frau Engel, who had studied voice at the famous Folkwang conservatory, and Brigitte Then-Zach, a fine pianist, had been blown by the winds of war into our small rural town and gave regular recitals, called 'Liederabende,' in the small ballroom of the Golden Lion, the local hotel. Owing to a great demand for cultural events and a dearth of performers after the war, their concerts were always packed.

There was no stage. A grand piano stood in the center of the ballroom with the audience seated in a circle around it. I always attended with my father and usually persuaded him to arrive an hour early just to get the best seats in the front row. The artists always wore the same black dresses, that of Frau Engel being floor-length and accentuated by a string of pearls. The two musicians represented to me the absolute epitome of beauty, class, and elegance. I adored them and would have done anything to please them.

That occasion came soon enough. At the rehearsal of a particularly passionate Wolf song, the piano, not having been serviced during the preceding thousand years of Nazi rule, gave out. Mr. Arndt, elementary schoolteacher and piano tuner, declared that several strings had broken and needed to be replaced. To get piano strings at a time when one could not even buy a simple nail posed a serious problem, which put future concerts in question.

That's when Mr. Arndt approached me with his plan to travel to Göttingen, the neighboring university town, where we would try to get the strings on the black market. For this we had to travel from the American into the British occupation zone, and a guileless looking schoolboy was needed to carry some extremely valuable, but illegal, contraband to market. My father's permission was obtained, and Mr. Arndt and I walked to the station to board the first departing train in the morning. In my satchel under piles of school books I carried several small jars full of butter, worth a fortune in those days, and my then still innocent looks got me through the military controls at the border and to Göttingen, where the black market was located close to the railroad station. By noon we had located a buyer, a war widow who was in greater need of butter than music. She led us to her house where Mr. Arndt expertly removed several strings from her Steinway, and we were on our way home.

Very late in the day and completely exhausted, we arrived at the Golden Lion. As a reward for the long day's work, I was given a glass of milk and two rolls, which I ate savoring every bite. Mr. Arndt enjoyed a beer while he installed the strings and tuned the piano. We were two very tired but content and happy smugglers. When he was done, he played in the almost dark ballroom a most beautiful piece that I had never heard before. He said it was the Moonlight Sonata by Ludwig van Beethoven.

Today, whenever I find a quiet hour, I like to retreat to a room in our house where we have installed a complex stereo system with various amplifiers, boxes, speakers, and other contraptions. It can be loaded with 250 discs simultaneously, and it allows me to select, by just clicking the remote control, Beethoven's Sonata No.14 in C-Sharp Minor, Op. 27, No.2. With another click of the button, I select Alfred Brendel, Vladimir Horowitz, or Rudolf Serkin to intone the first movement, *adagio sostenuto*, of the Moonlight Sonata. Sitting in total comfort, bathed in surround sound, listening to the world's premier pianists, I still think that some of the best music I ever heard was more than half a century ago, when Herr Arndt played just for himself and his youthful accomplice and when Brigitte Then-Zach and Frau Engel performed Schubert, Schumann, and Brahms in the Golden Lion in Witzenhausen.

February 26, 2003

≈

Confessions of a defrocked ballroom dancer

A charming Japanese movie, *Shall we Dance?* tells the story of a shy accountant who finds himself drawn to a beautiful young woman who teaches ballroom dancing to single men. Seen as a disreputable activity for a middle-aged professional man, he keeps his growing passion for dancing a secret from his family and co-workers. The movie provides both amusing insights into Japanese culture and delightful scenes of elegant ballroom dancing.

I rent the video occasionally and indulge in memories. In my youth, dance instruction was part of the ritual of growing up. At age seventeen, high school boys were teamed up with the girls in the class below them. The school hired dance teachers, who would teach us youngsters four standard formal dances—Vienna Waltz, English Waltz, Foxtrot, Polka—and three Latin American dances—Tango, Rumba, and Samba. After about ten long lessons, the course culminated in a formal ball to which our parents were invited, so that they could observe for themselves how much or how little grace and agility their monetary investment had yielded.

Dancing lessons were the watershed over which we boys crossed into manhood, at least in our own minds. Not very precocious and more restrained in our relations with the opposite sex than is often the case nowadays, dancing lessons for us meant early manhood. We felt terribly adult holding a young woman's body close to ours and being allowed to plant our hands on her, although the proper position of both hands was exactly prescribed. Should one of our hands, especially the right one, slip too low, it was sternly and unfailingly adjusted upwards by the instructor.

Being seventeen and very interested in girls, I preferred the dances that allowed for close physical contact. Vienna Waltz and Polka were fine, but they did not compare with the moody English Waltz or the sensuous Tango, which I liked to dance with a particularly attractive and curvaceous girl. Today I realize how very harmless and restrained all this was, and I am grateful that

156

no videos exist of my youthful and undoubtedly pathetic attempts to infuse my Tango with the erotic passion it demands of its aficionados.

But the educational goals of our instructors went beyond mere dancing. Proper manners had to be impressed upon the provincial young men. An ironclad rule demanded that no girl be left sitting. No matter how unglamorous, each girl had to be asked to dance. Every once in a while, our teachers declared 'Damenwahl,' at which time the girls selected their dance partners, thus letting the men experience the embarrassment of not being chosen.

Forty years later and looking for an entertaining form of exercise, my wife and I resumed ballroom dancing. Eager not to embarrass ourselves by exposing our rusty dancing techniques to a larger group, we rented a local dance studio and a private instructor two hours each week and threw ourselves into the arms of Terpsichore. But alas, the dancing fervor of my youth could not be recovered, and my wife proved to be the much better dancer. Our instructor had to dance a lot more with me than with her. I thought it was because I needed a lot more work than Carol did; she thought it was because the instructor was gay. Secretly she hoped a reporter from the student newspaper would click a photo of this dapper man dancing a passionate Tango with the WMU president.

Nevertheless, we were not spared embarrassment. When our lessons were over, we continued practicing at home. At the president's house we cleared out the garage, put a stereo system up and danced the night away working on the Tango. One night, while we were dancing, we heard uproarious laughter and noticed a dozen eyes watching us through the garage door windows. My daughter, having unexpectedly returned home from college with several friends, saw her old parents tangoing about in the empty garage with as much passion as they could muster at their age. It obviously was not enough. Ever since, we are content to watch Tango dancers only in the movies.

February 21, 2001

≈

Love, passion, heartbreak—my operatic past

Very few people know of my past as an opera singer. In fact, only when my wife recently brought order into a collection of old photographs, memories returned of a time when I graced the stage in an opera by Cesar Bresgen, entitled *The Hedgehog as Bridegroom.*

The opera's plot is a fairy tale: a lovely princess, having lost her way in the dense woods surrounding her father's castle, is helped to find her way back home by a hedgehog, but she must promise the thorny animal that she will marry him upon her safe return. Once back in the safety of the castle, the princess forgets her promise until one night, at the beginning of a festive banquet, the bell is rung at the front portal, and the hedgehog appears to claim the princess as his bride. Not surprisingly, the princess, having harbored thoughts of a more romantic and less hurtful corporal union, resists. The king, however—that would be I— reminds his daughter that promises must be kept and forces her to make good on her word. As the species-challenged, unequal couple enter the wedding chamber, and the princess no doubt ponders the problem of how to make love to a porcupine, the usual fairy tale metamorphosis takes place. The prickly hedgehog turns into a smooth-skinned prince, which changes the mind of the princess instantly. The love of a pure woman, even if reluctant, had lifted the evil spell put upon the prince by a wicked witch.

As lovers of opera will have to admit, the plot is no more silly than that of many other operas, but this opera's music was lovely. Nevertheless, all the way through the work one feels the dichotomy between beautiful sound and wooden libretto, a discrepancy that becomes even more apparent to him who has to sing those words. For instance, the opening lines of my grand aria at the beginning of the royal banquet were: "Bring in the pig's head, rosy and baked, and ladle on the sauces for better taste, and most important: don't forget to pour the golden beer into our goblets." I belted this aria out with all my soul and the full power of my lungs, but only a still half-starved German audience in post-

World War Europe could fully appreciate the culinary appeal and the beauty of these words.

The opera had been composed (1950) a few years before I was cast in it. After months of rehearsals, we toured the entire region with our production. I had a passable singing voice that had been trained for a few years and, as I said, Bresgen's music was quite charming. I was in my last year of high school, age 18, ready to enter university, and very much enjoyed the adulation that any young man singing on a stage encounters from pubescent girls in the audience. However, my own amorous interests focused on the young girl, two years my junior, who sang the part of the princess. I had fallen deeply in love with her. I don't remember her name, but I can still see her lying before me on the stage floor, looking up to me with her beautiful black eyes and her delicate features, clinging to my legs, and pleading with me not to push her into that brutish hedgehog's wedding bed. Oh, how my heart agreed with her plea! How I would have liked to pull her up to my youthful chest, assuring her of my protection and love! But neither the libretto nor my own better sense allowed this. So I suffered, especially since the young girl did not know nor ever learned of my juvenile infatuation. My best friend, to whom I confided my chaste passion, seriously maintained that any amorous relationship of mine with the princess would be incestuous, since I was her father, for Pete's sake. In time, I got over it.

Thus I entered the world of opera properly: with unbelievable plot, amusing libretto, broken heart, youthful passion, unrequited love, and beautiful music. These youthful memories are now reduced to a few fading photos in a seldom visited album, but the passion for the music is still alive.

September 18, 2002

≈

Reflections of a feminist grandfather

My aunt Alexandrine Haenicke was born in 1895. While her brothers could expect to attend the university and enter a professional career, her own goal in life, dictated by the conventions of the 19th century, should have been to find a husband whose children she would raise and who would take care of her. Instead, she decided to become a scientist, a most unrealistic career aspiration at that time. Nevertheless, although professors occasionally refused to lecture while a woman was present or escorted her out of their labs, she could not be deterred and eventually obtained a doctorate in Biology. She was one of the first women in Germany to do so. She never married but lived and worked all her adult life with her partner, a similarly accomplished woman mathematician. I considered them both my aunts and admired them greatly. I seldom came away from their house without a banknote tucked into my pocket. "For books," they said, but never asked me afterwards if the money had indeed been spent for educational purposes. They also concocted potent alcoholic beverages, mostly sweet liqueurs, which they began dispensing to me in modest quantities when I was sixteen, to prepare me, they said, for the unavoidable temptations of student life.

Tante Lex and Tante Dora were the first feminists I ever met, although the term was not in vogue at their time. Their professional careers were difficult. Papers in the sciences written by women were only reluctantly accepted. Therefore, Tante Lex published her papers and books under the male version of her name (Alexander) or simply used her first initial, assuming correctly that the publishers would surmise that A. Haenicke was male. In spite of their fine publications, both women taught on the high school, not the college level, as their male counterparts did. What impressed me as a young man was their complete intellectual and economic independence, their constant readiness to speak their minds on politics and women's issues, and their total lack of deference to males in a family of very strong-willed Haenicke men.

They also tried to advise me in matters of the heart, but usually poorly. When I introduced my American fiancée to them and made known my intention to move with her to the U.S., they had fundamental reservations. "You are no Albert Schweitzer," (he had gone to the jungles of Africa), they lamented, "and remember what happened to your Uncle Joachim." (He had been killed in a car accident in New York in 1928.) I generously overlooked their inaccurate picture of the topography and the dangers of the New World, because they loved my future wife who they expected would protect me on my dangerous excursion into the wilds of America. Meeting my wife had further strengthened their long-held belief in the natural superiority of women.

The example of these two beloved pioneer feminist aunts remains powerful among the members of our family. My sisters, my wife, my daughter, and my daughter-in-law all have pursued their own independent careers, which is a source of great pride to me. Now I am watching carefully over my little granddaughter Stefanie who is full of the energy I observed in my two aunts. A college fund is already started, future schools are scrutinized, books are read to her daily, and educational toys and experiences are provided *en masse* by parents, grandparents, and other relatives, just to set her on the right track from the earliest moment. To our delight, her vocabulary expands. Everyday she makes new and exciting discoveries. She is growing into an interesting little person. It was therefore with surprise that I noted her wishes for Christmas: a vacuum cleaner and a Barbie doll. And as for her current career plans? She tells us with great firmness that she wants three things when she grows up. She wants to be a Molly Maid; she wants to have a gold tooth; and she wants to live in a trailer. My aunts, no doubt, would advise her to aim a little higher. So there is work for us to do; but we have time. Little Steffi is only three-and-a-half.

January 9, 2002

∼

Father and son, from very different times

Mother's Day was always easy for me. I loved my mother dearly. She was a warm, compassionate, generous, selfless, and fun-loving woman, and it was natural to bring her flowers, a poem, or to hug and kiss her, and to tell her how much I loved her. Father's Day was much more complex. It would never have occurred to me to put my arms around my father or to tell him that I loved him. But every year, on Father's Day, I regret, more deeply than at other times of the year, that the conventions of his times and his upbringing did not allow for a more tangible show of mutual affection.

My father was born in 1882 when Bismarck dominated European politics, and when German men considered it a point of high honor to have served in the imperial army. My grandfather, a career officer in that army, died early, leaving his widow a very small pension and six children, all younger than ten years. The emperor saw to the education of his officers' sons. The five boys left home at age ten and were raised in rigid imperial military academies or similar schools maintained by royal princes or dukes. A few years ago, I visited the little provincial town at the foot of the towering and grim ducal castle in which my father spent his youth. Although he received a splendid education, his youth was defined by joylessness and poverty. I have a letter to his mother in which he pleads for a pair of socks and new underwear. Later, supporting himself by playing piano at social events, he attended the university, was highly decorated as an officer in WW I, and at age 38 married my mother, a beautiful girl twenty years his junior with whom he had eight children.

When I was born, he was already 53. Soon after, another World War removed him, and I was ten when he returned, dispirited and beaten, at age 63. The old world of honor and duty in which he had been raised had been destroyed by the Nazis whom he despised, and the hardships of the post-war period left no time for him to play sports with his children or bond with them on fishing or camping trips. But we went hiking, and he would discuss with me historical events, converse in French or English, explain mathematical problems, or quiz me on irregular Latin verbs. Being a typical teenager, I did not consider these trips with their heavy academic content fun events. Only today do I appreciate how much I learned while hiking with my father.

We also never had the proverbial father-son talk about the birds and the bees. But we came close when I was fourteen. While reading Livy with him, we came to a passage about a Roman courtesan which read: "Sua lubido sic accensa, ut saepius vires peteret quam viribus peteretur." I translated, somewhat freely but correctly: "She was so horny, that she wanted to sleep with men more frequently than men wanted to sleep with her." My father swallowed, blushed, and left the room to fetch himself a cup of coffee. When he returned, we went right on to the next paragraph. I knew I had scored. No more need for the bee talk.

I excelled in school and loved learning, which pleased my father very much. Although he never told me so, I knew he was secretly proud. Instead, he told me he worried about me. I was easy-going, gregarious, loved to court the girls and go dancing with them, and I enjoyed a beer with my friends. His own youth had been entirely different and had made him formal and stiff in his bearing, reserved, serious, and parsimonious. Considering me argumentative and given to rhetoric, he suggested that I study the law. When I chose literature instead, he pleaded with me to pursue something solid with which I could make my way in the world. His worries meant he cared deeply about me in his Victorian way which was not given to showing emotion. He came from a very different time, but on Father's Day I often wish it had been different, both for him and for me.

June 19, 2002

∾

Let's not admire the workaholic

When I was a young man and spent much time in Greece, I strolled one weekday morning through Athens to spend a few hours at my favorite spot on Mount Lycabettos which afforded a wonderful view over the city. On my way I passed by a used bookstore and noticed in the window a rare and early edition of Schiller's works at a price that was stiff for a struggling student but still far below its fair market price.

Within minutes, I decided to move to a cheaper hotel and to forgo taxis for the rest of my stay and to buy the costly edition instead. And so I did. When the purchase had been completed, I told the dealer that I did not want to lug the many volumes up to Lycabettos, and that I would pick up the parcel on my way home after lunch. That was not possible, he replied, because he had decided to close the store right after I left. Through my purchase he had earned enough money for the day, he told me, and he would take the rest of the day off. I was welcome to fetch the books the next day, when he would open his store again.

I have thought about that little anecdote often in my life when necessity, ambition, or pure insanity drove me to work long hours. But perhaps I did not think about this lesson often enough. When I was a young father, I held an office that often demanded ten to twelve-hour workdays, and it was not uncommon that I had left for the university before the children woke up and returned home after my wife had put them to bed. On many days I just saw them asleep.

One day, returning from a four-day lecture tour, I had brought both children a toy from the trip. They embraced me and said: "We didn't know that you had been out of town." That was my conversion point. If a four-day absence goes unnoticed by your children, you are shortchanging them and yourself. From then on it was parents' nights at school, watching the children's teams, building things with them, reading with them, practicing the multiplication tables, watching them play in the backyard, listening to and laughing at the jokes they brought home from school—all the things that are so enjoyable while they go on and that are so long remembered afterwards.

Why is it so hard to learn the simple lessons and not find the small and perhaps only true moments of happiness in life? We know that great satisfaction does come from our work and a fulfilling professional life. Moreover, we all need to put bread on our tables. But how much bread does one need? Does one's house have to get ever bigger? How many toys can a person really play with? And at what price do these luxuries come? Is time itself perhaps more precious than time spent to make all these acquisitions possible? Is time more valuable if spent on family, friends, and personal reflection rather than on increasing one's net worth?

I have met many people over the years who tell me with great pride that they are workaholics. It is meant to be a badge of honor and distinction that separates them from those others who come home without a briefcase full of paperwork, who do not sit up late into the night plotting the work for the next overloaded day, week, or month.

Workaholics are addicted—the very name suggests it—and like all addicts they bear the traits of excessive and uncontrollable behavior. Why would anyone consider addictive behavior praise-worthy and exemplary? I cannot. Knowing how fast life flows by, I rather feel sorry for the workaholic who seeks our approving admiration but who, in my eyes, shortchanges his own life and the lives of those around him.

I have yet to hear about the man who, on his deathbed, regretted that he did not spend more time at the office.

December 1, 1999

~

I still cry at funerals

1999 was a year of too many funerals. Too often I found myself attending memorial services, feeling weighed down by sadness and memories.

I have a hard time at these services because I still cry at funerals. They make me feel deeply sad, and I cry when I feel sad. I know that I am supposed to fall in with the rest of the congregation and delve into happy memories of the deceased, remember amusing anecdotes, and 'celebrate his life' rather than mourn his demise. Nevertheless, I mourn and wipe my eyes. I can't help it.

During these 'celebration of life' ceremonies, I think, most of us simply seek protection against the ungovernable power of grief and despair. We attempt to postpone the reality of the event, it seems, and thus often hear at open casket funerals that the deceased looks peaceful, as if he were only sleeping. We avoid the words 'death' and 'dying' and say instead that our friend 'has passed on,' 'has passed away,' 'is no longer with us,' 'has left us,' or 'has departed.' We focus our thoughts on laughter-filled moments of the past, emphasizing those memories that make the deceased seem once again alive before our inner eyes, rather than dead.

While I gratefully partake in the happy memories, I nevertheless realize with anguish that what has occurred is irreversible, and that the loss is permanent and irretrievable. These thoughts fill me with deep sadness, frustration, and sorrow; and I grieve.

165

But our modern society does not condone public grief and has remanded such emotions to the privacy of home and family.

In my student days, many moons ago, I lived for a few weeks among peasants in a remote village in Greece, the only person not born and raised there. At that time, a young woman in the house next door died of cancer. During her last hours, family, friends, and neighbors stood around her deathbed comforting her. When she finally died, the village women began to wail, her husband lamented throughout the night, and her parents' cries of grief were heard throughout the neighborhood. The death of this young wife, mother, daughter, and neighbor was a primordial event in which the entire community participated, and which arrested life in the village until after the funeral.

To this day I remember how deeply affected I was by the naturalness of this uninhibited display of grief and anguish. I had recently lost my father, a towering and central figure in my life. Our large family had gathered, and we had laughed a lot while remembering and recounting his lovable idiosyncrasies and foibles and our mostly happy moments with him. I had met his death with the prescribed civilized control of emotion which, I painfully realized, had prevented closure on my part.

I found that closure while I was alone and away from home. When death visited my young neighbor, I felt irresistibly drawn into the grief of that small Greek community and was, for the first time, able to give emotional expression to my own earlier loss. I grieved along with the village, without inhibition and without restraint. The joint grieving became a cathartic event. Our wounds had been cleansed by our tears and began to heal.

Ever since that experience I believe in the power of catharsis. When a loved one dies, the admonition to get over the past and to focus on the future is lost on me. Our past is as much part of us as is our present and our future. Our past, happy or mournful, never leaves us; it is never done with us. When I bury a friend, I must cope with the loss of our joint past—on my own terms. And that includes lots of tears.

February 25, 2000

≈

Did my wife understand her wedding vows?

This week my wife and I celebrate the anniversary of our wedding, which took place on the 29th of September 1962. We were married close to my boyhood home in Germany, and I remember well the glorious fall day and the romantic castle, perched high on a hill, where the ceremony and the wedding party were held. It is a blessing that my memory of the day is so vivid, because we have no real wedding pictures. The photographer, hired for the momentous occasion was a total incompetent who produced only a few blurred pictures that looked as if taken by a drunk. The ceremony in the little private chapel behind the castle was conducted by a German-speaking parson, which makes my wife claim to this day that she was not fully aware of what she promised when our vows were exchanged. My mother-in-law had the typical motherly reservations about her daughter's careless choice of a husband, but my father-in-law was happy, because the entire affair with elaborate meal, wines, flowers, parson, incompetent photographer, and rented castle cost him the equivalent of $400. That's how strong the U.S. dollar was 38 years ago.

Since then I have attended many weddings, most of them with deeper emotion and more reflection than I mustered at my own. When I married, I was thoroughly happy, free of any doubt, optimistic about our own joint future, and completely unknowledgeable of what would lie ahead. I was just like all the young people whose weddings I now attend, and who are just as happy and optimistic as I was then. Now I sit in church, with the experience of a long married life, and hear their vows, made in front of the congregation and in the face of God: "To have and to hold...for better or for worse...in sickness and in health...until death do us part." Every time these words are exchanged, I am deeply moved, and I pray that this man and this woman will find a love enduring enough to live up to such uncompromising, all-encompassing promises.

I sit in my pew and reflect on what these vows will mean in the lives of the newly wedded couples. Even the luckiest among them will have to face the unavoidable little irritations about each other's personal habits and likes; the occasional disparities in wants, in taste, in friends, or politics; the development of their partners in unexpected ways; and the transition of youthful passion into lasting affection and healthy dependency. But for some couples, harder challenges are waiting when fortunes or good health change. The young people before the altar never have the slightest idea where their adventurous journey will take them, and what monstrous dragons may lie in wait along the way. Raising the full sail of optimism, they leave harbor, our best hopes and wishes accompanying them.

The *Gazette* regularly shows couples who have been married for long periods, their original wedding picture juxtaposed with a recent photo. I love to view those snapshots: youthful, happy faces at the beginning of their marriages and beautiful, content old faces many years later. Between these two images lie untold, but epic stories of useful lives jointly built, children raised, mortgages paid, wars survived, laughter and tears shared, good luck and foiled hopes, success and failure—all of it borne together by two people, now old, but once young and hopeful, and all of it endured because of a man's and a woman's kept commitment and that rarest of gifts, their uncompromising love. I look at those faces often, and I recall the promises they once made to each other. And I know how fortunate I am to have found a woman who would have me; who stuck it out with me for better or for worse; and who, without wavering, stood at my side in sickness and in health.

Would it be different had the parson spoken English? No matter what my wife claims, she understood, and many times affirmed, every German word the parson spoke 38 long and happy years ago in that little chapel behind Berlepsch Castle.

September 27, 2000

≈

Coming to America through its front door

My European nieces and nephews hop on a plane in Frankfurt at the drop of a few hundred euros and arrive in Detroit or Chicago a meal and a movie later. Flying to the U.S. is no big deal for them. When I pick them up at the airport, I often remember how different my own first arrival in America was four decades ago.

I entered the country as millions of immigrants before me: legally, and by boat, sailing into the harbor of New York. Ocean liners were still the preferred mode of travel between Europe and America then (1963), and the five to seven days it took to cross the Atlantic cost much less than flying the same distance in about seventeen hours. My host, the Fulbright Commission, was willing to pay for either plane or boat, but my wife traveled with me, and the boat ticket beat out the cheapest airfare, offered by Icelandic Airlines.

A trip to America in those days still carried the aura of adventure. Family and friends would accompany the traveler to the pier, would be allowed to come on board and inspect the ship's amenities. Finally, several long whistle blows announced the pending departure, signaling all non-passengers to leave. Last embraces and tears, and the band would strike up a tune. Then we would stand at the railing for a long time, waving down to those at the dock, shouting some last greetings, while the ship was slowly tugged out of the harbor. There was a sense of finality in those departures. Those who left would not be back in a few days. The farewells were typically said for a long time.

Our quarters on the boat were not lavish. A lowly Junior Fulbright Lecturer (that was my classification) could only claim a cabin of very modest size, but as newlyweds we preferred narrow sleeping quarters to king-sized beds anyhow. Getting up in the morning, however, was another matter. The cabin was so narrow that one of us had to stay in bed and out of the way while the other one got dressed. The shower was the size of an upright coffin, just big enough to stand in, but almost too small to move one's hands up and down to apply soap. Still, boat travel was somehow elegant. One dressed for the evening table and other social occasions, and during the day, uniformed waiters pampered the passengers by serving drinks and tasty tidbits throughout the boat.

During the voyage, anticipation built up steadily for those who traveled to America for the first time. Would one find the country really as big, as ruthless, as horrible, or as beautiful as one had heard, read, or been told? Then, finally, came the day when we sailed into New York harbor, a highly emotional moment. After I saw the tip of Manhattan rising out of the sea, I could not go back below deck. Gliding past the Statue of Liberty and Ellis Island, I thought of all the generations of emigrants who had arrived before me, most of them under incredibly less comfortable conditions. But they had made the same journey, had seen the same first glimpses of this continent, and had probably been moved by just as much fear and hope on their arrival as I.

Arriving by boat in NYC was like coming through a front door which on its arch had inscribed in big, inviting letters: This is America. And behind that door lay Manhattan with its skyscrapers, its delis, its elegant stores, its cabbies and quicktongued waitresses, its music, its theaters and museums, its ethnic neighborhoods teeming with people from all over the world, with every shade of color, speaking languages one had never heard before. New York is not America, we all know it, but it was and remains a breathtaking and totally overwhelming first impression.

Times have become faster, and very few people today land by boat in New York. I am glad it was different when I first entered the country. A quick non-stop flight from Frankfurt to Detroit is just not the same.

October 24, 2001

∼

Women's lounges and other mysterious places

When I arrived in the United States in 1963, I felt linguistically well prepared. I had begun learning Oxford English in school when I was ten and was widely read in English literature. I was supremely confident.

Little did I know. What good does it do having read Shakespeare and Keats when you want to converse with a taxi driver in New York? I had heard it said that the English and the Americans are two nations separated by a common language. Never did this become clearer to me than during my first days on the shores of the New World.

Luckily, I had my American wife in tow. She saved me from misunderstanding, confusion, and potential harm while I negotiated my first cautious steps in America. I did not speak idiomatic American but translated literally from one language to the other. So she freed me from the fangs of immigration officials and handled conversations with curt waitresses and mumbling cabbies.

Nevertheless, my linguistic naïveté got me into trouble soon enough. Wanting to use the bathroom in a New York hotel, a staff member directed me to a door bearing the sign "Men's Lounge." Having been in a cocktail lounge earlier, I knew what a lounge was and found what I expected: a semi-elegant room with a sofa and a few chairs, mirrors on the wall, and a swinging door leading obviously into further rooms for lounging. Convinced that I had been misdirected, I left and explained my wants again to another waiter who told me to look for the 'Restroom.' However, resting was not what was on my mind either. I could have done that in the lounge, but more urgent needs had to be taken care of first. After further conversations with hotel staff, another waiter guided the now slightly panicky foreigner back to the men's lounge, pointed to the swinging door behind which to my astounded eyes all the installations presented themselves that were needed for the activities I was eager to pursue.

Years of English studies had failed me. I had not learned that in polite American society one goes to the bathroom, the restroom, the little boys' room, or the men's lounge 'to wash one's hands.' German restaurants give unmistakable directions. A large arrow in the back of the restaurants will direct one "To the Toilets"—plain and simple. And you don't go there only to wash your hands either. A country with very high per capita beer consumption is wise to avoid misleading signage when existential needs arise.

But 'Women's Lounges' presented similar mysteries for the novice immigrant. After my initial experience with the men's lounge, I realized that when women left the restaurant table to go to the lounge they were not expressing a desire to find other, more entertaining company. While men went 'to wash their hands,' I learned that women used their lounge 'to powder their noses.' What else?

I also noticed that women frequently left the table in groups to go to the women's lounge. One would get up, and unalterably another one would rise to join the expedition. Why did women go in pairs? What beyond the obvious did they do in the women's lounge? Plot strategy against their dinner partners? Share secrets that could not be mentioned in front of men? Every conspiracy theorist would have had a field day with this suspect display of female solidarity.

It was obvious to me that I could not act similarly. Suggesting to another man at the table to go to the men's lounge together would probably have been met, then and now, with raised eyebrows. I had discovered yet another area in which men were at a social disadvantage. There was for men no sanctuary equivalent to the women's lounge.

Later, the women's movement did away with powdered noses, and the joint strategy sessions in women's lounges subsided. I wonder why. It is one of the ironies of my life, that many women in Kalamazoo gratefully remember me as the man who ordered fifteen more stalls added to the women's lounge in Miller Auditorium.

Obviously, I can no longer be considered a conspiracy theorist.

February 16, 2000

Celebrating forty years of friendship and love

I called my friend Hubert in Germany to congratulate him on his 68th birthday. Aeons ago, we attended the University of Munich together, he in sports physiology, and I studying literature. We were at that time inseparable, good buddies. Hubert, a retired teacher, now lives in a small Bavarian town, and I cherish the thought that this good man is still my close friend after more than forty years.

Hubert always had an eye for the girls. He and I were both instructors in an American study abroad program in Munich, and he would scan all new students the moment they stepped off the boat. So he asked me one day if I had noticed "the little black-haired girl" among the new arrivals. 'Little' referred to the fact that we were about six years older than our students, which in our twenties made a great difference. Indeed, I had noticed the little black-haired girl also. She was the freshman daughter of the American program director of the institute at which Hubert and I taught. She seemed awfully young to an old Ph.D. candidate like me, but I fell in love with her nevertheless, and three years later we were married in a beautiful mountaintop castle surrounded by woods, close to my hometown in the midst of the Grimm Brothers' fairy tale country.

The little black-haired girl and I celebrated our fortieth wedding anniversary last week. Like all happily married couples, we can't believe how quickly the years rolled past; and like all happily married men, I would without a moment's notice go on that same journey again that was so full of wonderful surprises and blessings. Many of my friends, Hubert among them, divorced and took a second or third wife. I don't dare take any credit for it that my union lasted. I take it as one of my life's blessings.

When I talk to couples our age, I am always surprised how different life was for our generation. When we started out, we had very little but ourselves. For years we lived in small apartments, drove used cars, went to cheap double feature movies, stayed in very modest motels when we traveled, had potluck dinners with our friends, and still ran out of money by the 25th of each month.

But we had lots of fun, sat up and talked to our friends till the wee hours, and worked very, very hard.

Our material expectations were modest, and we were not plagued by unreasonable wants and ambitions. My wife never demanded things that a teacher's salary could not provide. While my income was small, we never considered ourselves poor or dissatisfied.

In the early years of our marriage, I immigrated to a foreign country, a very difficult adjustment for someone like me so steeped in German language and literature and European culture. My wife became my cultural guide, translator, and editor for years, while I tried to perfect my English and advance my American university career.

Later, she stalled her own professional plans to raise our two children without ever a word of complaint or regret. As I took to the American university system and moved around from one position to the next and from one university to another, I had a reliable, steadfast trooper at my side, who organized major moves, redecorated home after home, took care of all family affairs, managed our modest finances, negotiated with doctors, plumbers, teachers, roofers, babysitters, and car mechanics so that I could entirely focus on my teaching and research. In later years, when honors and recognition occasionally came my way, it was she who held my feet on the ground and kept me away from pomposity. During my many illnesses, hers was the hand I held until I was rolled into the O.R., and hers was the first face I wanted to see if I should make it back.

The little black-haired girl is a grandmother now, and her hair is not black anymore. But like thousands of other husbands, I remind myself every day of my enormous luck of having been chosen and accompanied for so many years by such a good woman.

October 2, 2002

≈

Old files open vistas on the past

One of my many New Year's resolutions was to clean out drawers, closets, and shelves and to finally become a real neat person. But why stop there? Soon my zeal for orderliness and creating more space spilled over into weeding out old files, a bittersweet and time-consuming activity since going through old files leads to revisiting one's life.

There is the mortgage taken out on our first house that cost considerably less than what I now pay for a new car. But then it seemed to us an immense sum of money. The bank insisted that we take mortgage insurance on my life. Relatives helped us with the required down payment. We were so proud of that very modest first home. And we raised our children in that house. Some final happy reflections, and out goes the mortgage.

Then come old pay stubs from my days as a struggling young instructor, and as I thumb through them I wonder how we ever made ends meet on that income. The stubs inevitably evoke memories of our young and happy marriage, "living on love, buying on time," as the popular song goes. I remember filling the tank of my old used Rambler with gas at 29 cents a gallon and taking Carol to the movies on Wednesday nights, when double features were shown for 75 cents a person. We made our popcorn at home and smuggled it into the movie hidden under our coats. How could we be so content with so little? A last look, a smile—and the stubs fly into the waste paper basket.

Class syllabi from my first courses follow. I feel once more the excitement of teaching my first graduate seminar, and I remember the faces and fates of some of my early students. Several of them are now full professors, teaching their own graduate seminars and writing better books and papers than I ever did. Did I have anything to do with that? I look at the syllabi one last time, find them brilliant, exciting, yes, inspired—and toss them out with the other papers.

Next a whole sheaf of student evaluations of my classes. Vanity overcomes me. I read them and they warm my heart, although I know deep down that students are overly generous in assessing their instructors when they feel the teacher loves what he teaches and loves those he instructs.

But before I put them aside, I remember one last time how very hard I worked for my classes and how carefully I prepared them. We lived in a blue-collar neighborhood in Detroit in those days with mostly automobile workers as our neighbors. They were wealthy people by our standards. Unlike us, they drove new cars, and many even had a boat in their driveway for fishing trips 'with the guys.'

I taught mainly in the morning and would sit the rest of the day on my front porch reading and thinking for hours on end. Some of my neighbors assumed that I was unemployed, always reading while other people pursued honest work. Occasionally, they would come by, beer bottle in hand, and let me know about openings at their plant. I told them what work I was doing at the university, but I began to read more surreptitiously inside my house. I also began to drink beer on my front porch in the late afternoon and shed my image as an 'egghead,' which was the term then used for nerds.

There are drawers full of photos, letters from friends and well-wishers, programs of graduations, funeral services, the children's school performances, festive dinners, and birth announcements of now married men and women. Is there a house without these drawers and boxes filled with fond and bittersweet memories? How much of our past can be conjured up by just one little piece of paper!

I decide to keep some of them for future sessions following future New Year's resolutions. I enjoy, on occasion, revisiting the past. After all: reminiscing is the vice of old men.

January 19, 2000

~

Happy Birthday card to Detroit says, "Get well soon!"

I love Detroit. And that's why I have to send her a birthday card while she celebrates, with great pomp, her glorious 300th birthday. Three hundred years is not a long time for cities such as Rome, Athens, London, or Paris. But in America, 300 years encompass more than the country's entire national history. It is a big, memorable birthday, indeed.

I was a Fulbright lecturer in 1963 and had to select a destination. I had offers from Haverford, Amherst, Austin-Texas, and the University of Michigan—but I chose Detroit, where my wife had grown up. With some interruptions, we lived there for the next sixteen years.

Detroit, at that time, was the quintessential American city: big, raw, industrial, hectic, productive, and energetic. Its art institute, its symphony, and its public library were cultural gems. Motown music was coming into its own. Cass Technical High School was a model for the nation. Working class neighborhoods boasted loud and colorful bars and cozy eateries. Ethnic restaurants—Jewish, Italian, Greek, Near Eastern, Polish, African-American—abounded throughout the city. Hamtramck and Greektown lured thousands of office workers to lunch. On summer evenings, we sat on Belle Isle and saw the ships go by on the mighty Detroit River, or we went to Tiger Stadium. When the Tigers won the World Series, the whole town went crazy with pride. It was a great city to live in.

My life was centered at Wayne State University, an urban university where many students were the first in their families to attend college. The school meant to Detroit what City College had once meant to New York: it provided an affordable, excellent education and put legions of immigrants, minorities, salesmen, policemen, waitresses, and sons and daughters of factory workers on the ladder of social advancement. I never again taught more attentive, demanding, and feisty students. Many were quite unsophisticated, but they wanted to learn and did not expect their teachers to motivate them. They demanded an education for their hard-earned money.

It was then that I fell in love with American public education. Unlike in Europe, I saw an educational system that disregarded family background and social status but was open and welcoming to everyone. The faculty was tolerant, progressive, extremely liberal, and, like their students, had strong ties to the labor unions. Many of my lifelong friendships—social, political, and academic—were formed during my years on that campus.

Racial tensions, however, were present throughout all those years. The battles for school desegregation were won, but they led to an accelerated exodus to suburbia. Riots and two decades of race-baiting political leadership further depleted whole neighborhoods. The exit doors of the city swung wide open, and nobody made any serious attempts to close them. When I finally left in 1978, the city had begun its downward slide from which it has not yet recovered.

When I visit Detroit now, I can't believe what has happened. I see formerly proud hotels and elegant downtown stores boarded up; the city's major arteries like Woodward, Gratiot, Grand River, or Livernois are blighted beyond belief; and once lively neighborhoods are studded with abandoned houses. Detroit has become the most racially segregated metropolitan area in the country, and the city's destructive obsession with race is almost tangible. Overwhelmed by insurmountable social problems and incompetent leadership, the school system ended up in receivership. Dennis Archer, the city's great hope and her best mayor in thirty years, leaves office exhausted, his grand dream of making Detroit a world-class city unfulfilled.

Each trip to Detroit is like visiting the sickbed of a dear, seriously ill old love with whom I shared the good times when I was young. Her body is racked by powerful maladies which seem to defy any cure: widespread poverty, crime, drugs, and divisive racial politics. Yet my nostalgic eyes still see her former beauty shine through her devastated features, and in my heart I know that there is hope for her. I pray you will recover, Detroit, my old love, and Happy Birthday!

August 22, 2001

~

Christmas Memories:

Camping with the Holy Family

Each December we celebrate the wondrous arrival of the Christchild, bringing into the world His heavenly light and the promise of our salvation. The simple joy of the miraculous birth has, in my family, put children at the center of Christmas as long as I can think back.

My mother, who had four sons and four daughters, was a genius when it came to heightening her children's anticipation of the holidays. Christmas began four weeks before the actual holiday with the first Sunday of Advent. The smaller children were sent to the nearby woods to collect fir branches, which my mother arranged decoratively and on which she hung little stars we children had crafted from straw. During the war years, the framed photographs of absent family members were also adorned with fir branches and moved into places where our eyes fell on them all the time.

From the finest branches my mother finally wove a large wreath and put four candles on it, one for each Advent Sunday. On the first Sunday, the first candle was lit; a second the next Sunday, until all four candles burned together on the last Sunday before the 24th. In the late afternoon, when the outside world grew dark, my mother would light the appropriate number of candles on the wreath, and we sat together for hours, singing Christmas songs in the dimly lit room, accompanied by my older sisters on the recorder or by my father on the piano.

In good times, there were Christmas cookies and lots of Stollen, a traditional German delicacy, half bread and half cake, laden with heavy, glazed fruit, sugar, and marzipan. My father prepared Glühwein, his favorite mulled red wine, and even the children were allowed to partake, with thimble-sized glasses, in this special holiday libation. When the candles had burned down and the lights were turned on again, we usually turned to handicrafts. My sisters embroidered or knit simple little presents, and I, with a tiny saw, cut scrap wood pieces into star-shaped candle holders, which became my Christmas presents for parents, uncles, and aunts. Unable to buy presents for my older siblings, I gave them vouchers guaranteeing my servitude for certain, time-limited services. I promised to take out the garbage or sweep the sidewalk in their stead for a month, or iron a specified number of blouses and skirts for my sisters. My older siblings, without fail and mercy, called in each one of my promised services, usually just when I wanted to run off to play soccer, and in May I often regretted the excessive generosity that had overcome me during the pre-Christmas season.

Now, sixty years later, our American house is beautifully decorated by my wife, who carries on her mother-in-law's sense of joyful wonderment which accompanies the Christmas season. The little boy I once was still loves all the little touches that make our home festive for the holidays.

But many things are different. I now have gardening services and drip-dry clothes, so my street-sweeping and ironing skills have become obsolete. Famous choirs and vocalists now sing the Christmas songs in our house via a superb stereo system. Only when alone in my car do I still sing German carols, loudly and with lots of nostalgia. The once so delicious, heavy Stollen has become hard on my stomach, and there is a self-imposed one-slice limit. More than one glass of mulled wine tends to give me a severe headache. The old joys are no longer what they used to be.

The new joys are the grandchildren whom I attempt to introduce to family Christmas traditions. My younger granddaughter is fascinated with the crèche we display. I have told her the Christmas story, as simply as one can to a two-and-a-half-year old. But she interprets our crèche her own way. She claims that the Holy Family, resting in open air under the stars, is on a camping trip. She insists that the three Magi are the three baby sitters. Obviously, there is lots of work to do.

But now, with grandchildren at my knee, I might start singing carols again, hopeful that sixty years from now the little ones will remember their childhood advent seasons with as much fondness as I do today.

December 25, 2002

≈

Peace on Earth—Christmas 1945

Christmas 1945 is the most wonderful Christmas that I remember. It is also the most desperate and impoverished in my memory. And, given the circumstances, that is not a contradiction.

On May 9th, 1945, a few days prior to my birthday, the German armies had unconditionally surrendered, and the Third Reich had ceased to exist. The church bells rang for hours, telling us there was peace. At ten years old, I could not remember what peace was like. When asked, my mother told me that we could now sleep each night in our own beds without moving into air raid shelters, and that our family would live together again.

And indeed, in the following months, fathers, uncles, older brothers, and sisters came home from the war, one after the other. No telephone or mail existed to announce their return. Scraggy, exhausted, and half-starved, they suddenly turned up, many unable to believe that they had survived. A small country road led to our town, and we children would interrupt our games each time a figure showed up on the horizon, silently observing its approach and hoping it would be a returning relative. When trains with German prisoners of war passed through, we went from one wagon to the next holding pictures of family members and calling out their names in case someone might know their whereabouts.

Our family was among the lucky ones. My father had returned, and of the eight siblings, seven were accounted for. Only one older brother had not come home by Christmas, but we had word that he had been seen alive in a Russian prison camp. The winter was harsh. The U.S. army had requisitioned our house, and our family had to evacuate it within just a few hours. Clutching our few belongings, the seven of us stood helplessly in the streets, till an angel appeared in the form of Frau Marb, a neighborhood seamstress, who invited us to live with her in her tiny flat. It was so small that all of us could not even sit down at the same time. Quickly, space was created in her underground cellar where the laundry was usually boiled in a big kettle, and where the year's supply of coal and potatoes was stored. The cellar was swept, sheets and blankets were hung to create visual privacy between the various cots, chamber pots, and ewers, and my mother and Frau Marb attempted to convince us children that this was all a big adventure.

The Advent season was filled with love, and we felt close and strong and safe as a family. A small Christmas tree was brought in from the wooded hills surrounding our town. In the evenings we fashioned decorative straw ornaments and paper garlands for the tree while my older sister played the recorder and we joined her in singing carols together. We talked much about my brother in Russia. My father would read to us by candlelight, introducing us to the great works of literature. He had become a stranger to me, just as my older siblings had, whom I had seen only sporadically during the war. Peace had made us a family again.

I don't remember any presents. I only recall that I kept for Christmas a culinary delight, three Hershey bars given to me by a kindly GI. I stored them for weeks in a sealed tin can, thus protecting them from both the ubiquitous mice and my own temptation. The chocolate was my contribution to our holiday feast. And I remember our Christmas dinner. Frau Marb and my mother, two saints who performed one miracle after the other, had produced out of their empty cupboards meat, potatoes, and gravy, and they even had found flour, sugar, and lard to produce the best Christmas cookies I ever tasted.

Many other warm family Christmases followed. The war was almost forgotten when my brother returned, eleven years later, from the prison camp in Siberia. But that first Christmas, when peace had returned to us, comes to mind every year, and, each time, the angelic message 'Peace on Earth' touches me deeply.

December 26, 2001

≈

Christmas in Vienna

At Christmastime, I like to be at home, and that means being with family and in a place I know, with warmth and comfort, and surrounded by my own things.

Only once in my life have I thought differently. My cousin Willi and I had jointly discovered, as many self-absorbed young men do, that our families were just too intruding and did not respect with proper sensitivity the personal space we two debonair men of the world needed. Seeing ourselves as grown men, we felt the urge to flee the disdained embraces of uncles and aunts, as well as the mulled wine, spiced breads, and other burdensome family traditions that we felt rested heavily on our youthful shoulders. Fancying ourselves as reasonably cultured, we had chosen Vienna for our Christmas sojourn, expecting that Christmas markets, opera and ballet, and the midnight bells of the Stephans-Dom would serve as the fitting background to our quest for youthful independence.

Vienna was glorious. We chose a hotel not far from the opera and with enthusiasm and gluttonous curiosity explored the city, never giving the approaching holiday much thought. When Christmas Eve finally arrived, we made reservations for dinner near the hotel, savoring our worldliness and suaveness. But around 9 p.m., the dining room emptied out, the waiters began to dim the lights and rustle glasses, silverware, and chairs as a subtle indication that our welcome had come to an end. It was time to go home to family, spouses, and sweethearts and to celebrate Christmas.

We left reluctantly and set out to find a cozy wine restaurant or some such other entertainment appropriate for two small town fellows ready to embrace the big city. But the big city was not ready for our embrace—not that evening. Wherever we entered, the establishment was about to close, the last call for orders having been issued long ago. Vienna was assembling inside warm family homes, leaving outside all those who did not belong. Our last hope was the hotel, but the friendly receptionist had gone home and had been replaced by a surly woman who responded to our request for service with a pitiless and indignant smile. This is Christmas Eve, she seemed to think, why are you hicks not at home where you belong? But for a tip approximating a bribe she turned on one lonely light in the deserted bar and put a bottle of wine on a corner table where Willi and I settled in.

Among my Christmas presents for Willi were two beautiful decks of cards. We were both masters of Skat, a card game played in German-speaking countries, which we had learned to play to perfection riding on school buses throughout the years. But Skat needs three players. The surly woman, mellowed by yet another bribe, found us a maintenance worker in the bowels of the hotel who was willing to be our third man. As men of the world and in the spirit of Christmas we assured him that we would replace his financial losses, should there be any. For about two hours, Willi and I played our best game. At the end, there was no restitution to be made to the maintenance man, who had taken us to the cleaners. The spirit of Christmas had not visited him. He kept our money.

At midnight we listened sadly to the church bells from all over Vienna and in our loneliness talked about past Christmases, remembered the smell of mulled wine and spiced breads emanating from the kitchen at home, and we very much missed the warm embraces of our family, overwhelming aunts and uncles included. We felt like calling home to tell our family how much we longed for them, but of course we didn't. We were still too insecure or too young, or both, to show our emotions to those whom we needed and loved.

I have learned my lesson. Understandably, I have given up playing Skat. And on each Christmas I stay home, drink mulled wine, and bestow my embraces on all those I love: family and friends and the probably embarrassed younger generation. Vienna can wait till spring.

December 26, 2001

≈

Biography

Diether Haenicke was born in Germany in 1935 and emigrated to the U.S. in the early 1960's.

He has worked in higher education for over forty years, serving as a professor, department chair, dean, vice-president, provost, and university president.

Haenicke earned his doctorate (*magna cum laude*) in literature and history at the Maximilians University (Munich) in 1962, was twice a Fulbright scholar, and taught at the University of Freiburg, Wayne State University, Colby College, and The Ohio State University.

He is the author of over 200 papers, reviews, articles, and books on literature, history, academic administration, international study, and educational finance.

After serving thirteen years as president, Haenicke now teaches and writes as a distinguished university professor at Western Michigan University. He and his wife Carol, their two children, and their families all live in Kalamazoo.

Since 1999, Dr. Haenicke has published a weekly column, appearing every Wednesday, in the *Kalamazoo Gazette*.

To order additional copies call the Kalamazoo Gazette at 1-269-388-2710 or visit the Gazette store at www.gazettestore.com